M000086253

PATH TO FREEDOM

Christian Experiences and the Bible

JEAN CORBON
TRANSLATED BY VIOLET NEVILL

The St. Paul Center Studies in Biblical Theology and Spirituality
SCOTT HAHN, GENERAL EDITOR

SERVANT
BOOKS

PUBLISHED BY ST. ANTHONY MESSENGER PRESS
CINCINNATI, OHIO

Nihil Obstat: Brendan W. Lawlor
                        Censor Librorum

Imprimatur: +Robert F. Joyce
                        Bishop of Burlington
                        January 2, 1969

The *nihil obstat* and *imprimatur* are official declarations that a book or pamphlet is free of doctrinal or moral error. No implication is contained therein that those who have granted the *nihil obstat* and *imprimatur* agree with the opinions expressed.

Cover design by Michael J. Frazier
Book design by Phillips Robinette, O.F.M.

ISBN 0-86716-616-9

Library of Congress Catalog Card Number 69-16993

This book was originally published in French under the title *L'expérience Chrétienne dans la Bible*, copyright © 1963, Desclée de Brouwer, Paris.

Servant Books is an imprint of St. Anthony Messenger Press.

St. Anthony Messenger Press
28 W. Liberty Street
Cincinnati, OH 45202-6498
www.AmericanCatholic.org
Printed in the United States of America

04 05 06 07 10 9 8 7 6 5 4 3 2 1

CONTENTS

INTRODUCTION TO THE ST. PAUL CENTER STUDIES IN
BIBLICAL THEOLOGY AND SPIRITUALITY

Scott Hahn, General Editor

The St. Paul Center Studies in Biblical Theology and
Spirituality are a series of books designed to help Christians
in their study of the Word of God. Dr. Scott Hahn serves as
general editor, and the St. Paul Center for Biblical Theology,
founded by Dr. Hahn, cosponsors the series with Servant
Books.

Each volume helps to fulfill the mission of the St. Paul Center,
which is to promote life-transforming study of Scripture in
the Catholic tradition. The Center serves clergy and laity, stu-
dents and scholars, with a variety of research and study tools,
from books and publications to multimedia programs and a
fully stocked Web library. All efforts promote an integrated
study of the Word of God: the Old Testament with the New;
the Bible within the liturgy; Scripture illumined by the tradition and the Magisterium.

We believe that every generation of disciples should know
Jesus in the breaking of the bread (see Lk 24:13-37) and
exclaim, as his first-generation disciples did: "Did not our
hearts burn within us while he talked to us on the road, while
he opened to us the Scriptures?"

FOREWORD

Few Catholics know the name of Jean Corbon, though many millions know his work and thousands of his words rest anonymously on the shelves of men and women in every parish in the world. Indeed, the Church has given his words a doctrinal authority held by very few theologians in all of history.

Father Corbon was the principal author of the fourth and final part of the *Catechism of the Catholic Church*, "Christian Prayer." Cardinal Joseph Ratzinger, in his essay, "Introduction to the Catechism of the Catholic Church," tells the dramatic story of Father Corbon's contribution:

> After having resolved to add a distinct fourth part on prayer to the first three, we looked for a representative of Eastern theology.... [W]e settled upon Jean Corbon, who wrote the beautiful concluding text on prayer while in beleaguered Beirut, frequently in the midst of

> dramatic situations, taking shelter in his basement in order to continue working during the bombardments. (*Introduction to the Catechism of the Catholic Church*, Joseph Cardinal Ratzinger and Christoph Schönborn, San Francisco: Ignatius Press, 1994, p. 23)

Some scholars see Father Corbon's influence extended beyond that last quarter of the book to the *Catechism*'s subsection, "The liturgy—work of the Holy Trinity" (*CCC*, #1077-1112), which echoes the language and thought of his book, *The Wellspring of Worship* (New York: Paulist Press, 1988).

What is it that makes Father Corbon particularly useful for the Church and for Catholics today? He spoke in terms that are personal, scriptural, liturgical, covenantal, ecumenical. All of these currents run strong and clear in the book you have at hand, *Path to Freedom: Christian Experiences and the Bible*. Father Corbon first published the book in 1963, when he was in his thirties. But it is a mature work of spiritual interpretation of the Bible—and spiritual direction of the reader. It is a remarkable work of biblical theology that leaves every reader richer and no reader unchanged. That is why we at the St. Paul Center, and Servant Books, chose *Path to Freedom* as the third title in our ongoing series of "contemporary classics" that offer intelligent, accessible Catholic study of Scripture.

Here, Father Corbon tutors us in "spiritual exegesis"—the Church's traditional method of reading Scripture "with its divine authorship in mind" (see Vatican Council II,

Dei Verbum 12). He firmly establishes the literal-historical truth of a biblical text, and then he helps us to discover its spiritual significance in our own life. For all of us, the Bible finds its fulfillment in Christ, whose incarnation represents the divinization of our human nature and whose life gives meaning to all human experience. Father Corbon puts it succinctly: "The Bible expresses Christ's—and hence our own—experience."

The book manages to cover all of salvation history, from the first moment of creation to the apocalyptic consummation in the heavenly liturgy. Each moment in the history of God's people corresponds to a moment in our own experience. In one of the more brilliant passages in the book, Father Corbon shows us how Israel's enslavement in Egypt represents our own enslavement by original sin, and thus how the parting of the Red Sea represents our own liberation through the waters of baptism. Our actual sins, however, correspond to Israel's exile in Babylon; now, our liberation requires a personal conversion, a decision to turn homeward through repentance.

Reading the Bible with Father Corbon, we come to know it as not only the Church's book but our book—your book and my book. The Bible tells a story. It is the story of God's people, yes, but it is also the story of each person. And since it was authored by God, who is almighty and all-knowing, it was written with each person specifically in mind. God never forgot any individual when he inspired Scripture, but we are free to forget this fact. And if we do, the Bible becomes meaningless to us. Spiritual reading of Scripture "is only possible," says Father Corbon, "if the reader is animated by the breath of the Spirit who gives life to the body of Christ."

Surely, it is the same Spirit who gave life to Father Corbon as he wrote the words of this book and, many years later, the words that would be enshrined in the *Catechism*.

Path to Freedom was written in Father Corbon's youth—in the 1960s—and it does bear some of the distinguishing marks of that provenance. There are obligatory mentions of existentialist philosophy, Freudian and Marxist analysis, evolutionary theory, and the documentary hypothesis of the Pentateuch—ideas whose time has all but receded. Yet neither they nor their obsolescence affect the central arguments of the book. We find similar idiosyncratic notions when we read the Church Fathers; but we do not dismiss Clement of Alexandria for his dogmatic vegetarianism or his frankly odd theories of human milk production. Father Corbon's book bears some marks of his time, but that is surely because he so passionately engaged his time, in the name of Jesus Christ.

Not many have known the joys and sorrows of the last generation as intensely as Father Corbon. He served as a translator and theologian at the Second Vatican Council, and he was active and influential in the most fruitful ecumenical efforts of the last generation. Indeed, in his life he showed forth the rich possibilities of a unified Christian church. A native of Paris, a western Catholic, he chose to make his home in the east. A member of the Dominican community of Beirut, Lebanon, he was a priest of the Greek-Catholic eparchy of Beirut. A faithful Christian, he persevered heroically in interfaith dialogue while living in a land torn by interreligious warfare.

Now, as his words are read in so many Catholic households, may his name become a household word for those who read the Bible. He has earned our closest attention.

Scott Hahn, Ph.D.
General Editor

PREFACE

The ideas developed in this book are based on the fact that the Old Testament is the pedagogue which leads us to Christ. In the Old Testament, God has revealed his pedagogy which, later, he was to bring to fulfillment in the Spirit of the risen Christ. Through a study of the *chronological stages* of the Old Testament, we shall try to recognize the *logical and vital stages* of our experience of Christ. This is not, therefore, a work of exegesis or biblical theology but rather an initiation into a spiritual reading—that is, a reading in the Spirit—of the Bible in its entirety.

Our whole life consists in living Christ, that is, in loving. For love is someone, the fullness of personal being: God. Christ is that love which permeates our whole life. In an attempt to express this wonder, one refrain will recur constantly throughout these pages, that of *gratuitousness*. Gratuitousness is the quality which marks the limpid love of the adult who loves another for himself and not because he finds in him the satisfaction of an egoistical need. We can act gratuitously when, liberated from the bonds of our own self-seeking, we can pour ourselves out in the spontaneity of self-giving. But we are capable of such love only if we have first received it by being loved gratuitously. There can be no free giving without free receiving. And herein lies the drama of gratuitousness: we have to consent to be loved by him and so be capable, in our turn, of loving as he loves, freely. "You have received freely, give freely" (Mt 10:8). "Let us love since He has loved us first" (1 Jn 4:9).

Before being written, this book has been lived by lay people, Christians for whom the Bible was once a closed book or, at best, was limited to a few of the more accessible pages of the New Testament. It bears witness to their passage from a faith still encumbered by rationalism to faith in the Lord Jesus within the freedom of the Church and a realistic appreciation of the drama of human life. In gratitude, this book is for them and for all those who are following the same path.

Mount Lebanon
Feast of the Transfiguration, 1962

INTRODUCTION

*THE HUMAN CONDITION
AND THE
EXPERIENCE OF CHRIST*

The Human Fact Is a Journey, a Passage

Man stands upright. The sap of life, springing from the depths of the centuries, has brought forth fruit from the earth. And each one of us in the period that takes him from his mother's womb to his first steps has lived through these first stages of development to become a man standing upright. But what of the living man? Our human condition is acted out between these two terms: that of a man standing upright to that of a living man. From the first manifestations of life to its fulfillment is one long passage in which we take possession of ourselves.

We want to be living men, to live life in its fullness, to fulfill ourselves. Once our youthful illusions are behind us and we have faced up to the reality of life, we find ourselves disappointed or stranded and lonely, but we still want to become living men. Camus once said that the only philosophical problem of any importance was suicide.

Disillusionment, apathy and distractions all betray with equal force that underlying desire to become living men. But what does this mean?

Shortsightedness is the most widespread affliction. Often we are aware of only one level of our existence: conditioned reflexes, biological needs, our work as transformation of matter, the betterment of society. We are capable of virtually isolating these levels from each other, acting out the part of our social self or of our intimate self, allowing ourselves to be "lived" like impersonal objectives or revealing ourselves as original subjects. But in no one of these ways can we really fulfill ourselves. There can be no partial fulfillment of man.

For we are a whole, a unique, disconcerting, polymorphous whole which cannot be reduced to any one of its component parts. We are in mutation, and now more than ever before, we have to face up to the necessity of integrating the totality of our human condition. That is what makes our time both so exciting and so tragic. In this tremendous thrust of the cosmos toward consciousness, we have reached a point at which shortsightedness becomes equivalent to suicide. We can no longer afford to ignore even the most obscure element of the human fact. Modern man, overwhelmed by his own wealth of being, must bring it to fruition or perish.

But when we try to grasp our human condition with our minds and realize it in our deeds, we see that it is paradoxical in its different aspects. We are a cluster of *complexities* in search of *unity*. This is true to a certain extent of all the different beings of the cosmos. But what is proper to man is that it is up to him to achieve his own unity from within himself. The different areas of our personality, from the conditioned reflexes falling within the realm of the physical sciences to the highest values falling within the domain of theology, can only be brought to their proper fulfillment in an ascending harmony. The unity of man will be attained only on arrival at a peak, after a long pull upward. And this upward movement comes from *within* man. In other beings the parts of the whole determine that being. In man those parts are both *determining* and *conditioning*: the way remains open for a higher adventure.

Hence the variations on our paradoxical theme. We are *individuals*, objective results of many necessary causes, and yet we are *persons*, unpredictable subjects ever moving onward. We are bound into a *collectivity* of various patterns, but we can only become ourselves in a *community* that knows no bounds. We live in the *present*, as do all bodies immersed in movement, but we are capable of taking time into ourselves and of living a *history*. We are part of the world of objective *phenomena*, but we are far more than we appear to be; we can be understood only by other personal subjects who enter into communion with our *mystery*.

At each moment the drama of man standing upright lies in the fact that he can only fulfill himself in *gratuitousness*. A civilization of leisure, the grip of ideologies (even those which are pessimistic), the disinterested dedication to a cause, the desire for human betterment as well as the incurable vulnerability of men's hearts to authentic love—all this proclaims the human paradox: gratuitousness, that which frees us from all necessity, is *necessary* to man if he is to become a living man.

The dynamic elements that go to make up man can describe the human condition. They can never delimit or exhaust it. Were it only because man preexists and is interior to his own reflection on himself, he can lay hold of only a shadow of himself while the reality has already fled beyond his grasp. Man cannot be pinned down. He is always *moving on.* If an evolutionary theory of man is accepted by even the most cautious thinkers to be the most probable hypothesis, it seems too that, at least since the beginning of the historical era, man is the only branch of the tree of life that is still pursuing new adventures. It has been said that we have barely left the Neolithic age. The knowledge of this insofar as it appears to be founded on fact should suffice to make modern man aware that he is in a state of mutation.

THE FACT OF CHRIST IS A PASSOVER, A PASCH

But a fact came about in this evolution of neolithic man, and that fact is Christ. If we wish to understand this event, we must in all honesty place ourselves within it, seeing it, that is, both as a phenomenon and as a personal mystery. Too many Christians, nourished by religious rationalism instead of drinking deeply from the fountains of history, have made of Christ either a "great master of the past" with a purely moral influence in the present or an ideal "value-system" in the present but with no effective hold on history.

The Christ-event is the event of human complexity being totally integrated in unity. Christ is that being in which all that is human is caught up and brought onto the level of the personal and the gratuitous. In him gratuitousness is no longer a catalyzing value, but someone. And personality is no longer the frontiers of fulfillment but the fullness of all beginnings: God. Christ is the event in which a man comes to total fulfillment because God has taken him to himself, personally.

Shortsightedness in this context would consist in seeing this event from a purely objective and static point of view. But the elements that go to make up the human condition are dynamic. Man is in passage. This passage, which is the focal point around which unfold all the stages of human becoming, is called in Christian terms the Passover or pasch. Christ is a paschal event. He is more than this. He is the pasch totally accomplished in the life of a man. In him the human paradox is resolved not by elimination of the antitheses but by their being taken up into himself.

This great mutation of man is accomplished by Christ in his resurrection. When he rises from the bowels of the earth, it is no longer simply man emerging upright from mother earth, but now it is the living man who emerges; man who has broken through the barrier of death. In this emergence all our variations are resolved in harmony, everything passes from death to life.

Jesus Christ knew our mortal human condition in reality and not simply in appearance. He has gone through all the absurdity of that mortal condition which arouses us to revolt or to complacency. He has borne the weight of disillusionment that has given rise to existentialist thought and that stamps as vanity all our human efforts so rich with promise. Not only has he borne all this, but he has done so with a keen consciousness that the most lucid amongst us attain only fleetingly. But disillusionment is the conclusion that impotent reason reaches. In Christ there is no such thing: "he could read men's hearts" (Jn 2:25) and is the victim of no illusions. But he brings what is in man to fulfillment. Our radical incapacity to bring our own rich *complexity* into a balanced unity is burst open, in Jesus, to bear a lasting fruit. Everything in the risen Christ becomes *unified* under the thrust of a pacifying and victorious interiority.

He is the man in whom all the dormant possibilities—cosmic, biological and psychological—are re-created from within by the fullness of the personal "I" of the Son of God. This is the meaning of his risen body, the real body of a man, becoming totally transparent to his interiority: the power of life in which determinisms give way to the free play of spontaneity; a means of communication without barriers or exteriority; the focal point of a communion in which we "know" him by existing in him whilst becoming the best of ourselves. Jesus risen, freed from the *determinisms* of our mortal condition, is thus open to a new adventure, higher than anything our present state of evolution could ever have led us to dream of: the fullness of the living God.

Another paradox which is resolved in Christ is that of the individual and the person. *Individuality* makes each of us a necessary result; by it we are in fundamental opposition to, because distinct from, each other. Christ went through this also. His first condition in this world was limited, as is ours, by race, climate, language, food, means of travel, social constraints, suffering and death, not to mention the limits of his human knowledge and the subtle currents of his feelings.

Passing beyond death he brings all these riches and all these limitations to fulfillment in his *personality* which is now the source of freedom. He is no longer a "living soul" but a "life-giving spirit" (1 Cor 15:45). He has become the free-flowing fountainhead, the creative source, receiving and giving, always present and never a disappointment for the personal focal points that we too are.

Similarly, the bonds of *collectivity*, a heritage of our biological origins, are transfigured and become a call to communion with others. In the risen Christ a new body is born in which the personalities involved are, at the same time, the most fully autonomous and the most closely bound in love. Henceforth, the power of *communion* of the risen Christ with all human beings knows no limits in extension or in depth. Never has a dream of brotherhood and love been realized to this degree.

The same breaking of bonds can be seen in what concerns time. The living Christ has not escaped from time. On the contrary, he is present in time in all its duration and in all its richness. Time for him is no longer that fugitive *instant* of consciousness which our capacity for illusion always tends to exaggerate; it has become the fullness of presence. In all psychological truth the consciousness of Christ is coextensive with all of *history*.

On the other hand, if our human condition seems to be divided between the *phenomenon* of the personage that we appear to be and the *mysterious* reality that includes everything from the unconscious to the supra-conscious, it is true to say that the risen Jesus has resolved this theatrical paradox. In him all the dark shadows of the "persona" disappear in the light of the person. For him there is no longer either phenomenon or mystery; simply he IS.

Finally, the greatest force of attraction for man standing upright, gratuitousness, has become the new world of the risen Christ. In our present condition death represents all the combined forces of the inevitability, the absurdity and the failure of life. The euphemisms of ancient languages have often used the same root to express death and implacable destiny. Alongside the necessity of existing, that of dying is the only one that is self-evident. The risen Christ has taken both into himself in the gratuitousness of living. He is man, freed at last, for whom the flexibility of action is no longer labor nor repose but in whom love has become the breath of being and time, the leisure to be one's self.

CHRIST AND THE UNITY OF THE CHRISTIAN EXPERIENCE

If we pause to wonder where the creative power of our Christian experience comes from, the most immediate evidence leads us to reply: from living people who have handed it on to us. This milieu of living people is the Church. If we want to test the authenticity of this living transmission of the Christian experience which is tradition, we must refer to those who were the first to live the experience of the risen Christ and who, having proclaimed it in their words and by their lives, wrote it down. The Gospels and the apostolic writings preserved in the New Testament are thus a touchstone.

But it is important to note that the essential content of these writings and of the living preaching that they reflect can all be summed up in the one phrase: the event of the risen Christ. The starting point of their new life lies in that "It is true, the Lord has risen" (Lk 24:34). When Paul has to answer for the novel stand he is taking in front of a Jew, King Agrippa, the Roman officer who explains the case shows that he has seized upon the heart of the matter when he says: "They [that is, the Jews] only have a quarrel with him about some question of their religion and about someone called Jesus who is dead and whom Paul claims is living" (Acts 25:19).

The whole gospel proclaims this unheard-of event: a man has "made it." He has passed beyond death. He has succeeded in becoming totally living. This is no mythical adventure of a new Prometheus. We know enough not to be taken in by such fables even if they are told anew in modern jargon. The novelty of the event lies, on the contrary, in the fact that man did not get there all alone. The risen Christ is, inseparably, both the event of God and the event of man in the purest gratuitousness. Man's entrance into victorious life is God's entrance into man. The power of the gospel lies hidden in a mysterious alliance which every human being searches for in the obscurity of his own heart and which breaks out into the open in the risen Christ: God and man share a common destiny.

This event can be known in itself through reading the Gospels and through the living tradition. But we can only enter into a true knowledge of it when we live by it. If the human condition as it is lived now and in its totality cannot be reduced to the condition of an object, how much more is this true of the human condition brought to fulfillment in the risen Christ. To be nothing more than an object is to be capable of being known and grasped from without. But the human

11

condition can only be grasped through a living experience within which we are involved. For the risen Christ we must go even further: Jesus, whom no power could keep hidden in a tomb, is today living and life-giving. And the fullness of this event will always burst out from the bonds laid upon it when the gospel is reduced to the level of an abstract rule of life. If it is true that Christ has risen from death, then it is evident that his influence is a personal and not simply an ideal one; that it is present and not past; accessible to all human beings and not restricted to those nearest to him; present in all its fullness at each instant and throughout history; totally real in the unity of the phenomenon and the mystery.

The heart of the Christian experience, therefore, is *the present reality of the person of Jesus Christ* in whom the fullness of God and the fullness of man are united. And since Christ is the human pasch fulfilled in God, the Christian experience is the experience of that pasch. The Lord is risen. His pasch can be ours at each moment of our mutation. But in order to live this we must have a true understanding of two of the constituent elements of our experience: the solidarity in time, which is the fabric of historical unity, and the solidarity amongst persons, the fabric of the human community. Nietzsche made the comment that he might have been persuaded to believe in their God if the Christians of his time had looked a little more "risen" themselves. But we are risen beings if we really live by Christ. The fullness of personal gratuitousness has invaded the cosmos at one point in time, at one point in the human phenomenon: the risen Christ. This is why Christ's pasch can become at every moment and for everyone the supreme pasch of the cosmos and of humanity.

We can thus resolve the paradoxes of our human condition if we take them into ourselves in a way analogous to the way in which Christ has taken them into himself. We shall study the unfolding of this liberation in the following chapters. But we must realize that we do not live it simply by imitating Christ. We would deny history if we reduced Christ to the role of a model and saw the resurrection as being set in a given moment of time in the past. No. To live Christ's pasch means to enter into it personally at the moment in time in which we are living because it fills the whole of history, and we are in a very real way contemporary with it. For us, salvation—the passage that takes us from the condition of the man standing upright to that of the living man—is a drama that is always new with the inexhaustible novelty of the Christ-event. This extraordinary experience was spoken of by the Lord's first witnesses: "Even if we knew Christ in the flesh, we do so no longer. When a man becomes a new creature in Christ, his old life has disappeared, everything has become new about him" (2 Cor 5:16-17). The gospel is not, first and foremost, the book that relates this. It is an event of salvation, a new joy. This is the Christian experience, and it is the integral human experience.

But how in practice do we make the link between Christ's pasch and ours in him? In accord with the twofold solidarity mentioned earlier, present in time and in the mystery of personal beings, we can better understand the power of reality that is represented by that "living milieu" in which the risen Christ lives: the Church. In technical terms the Church is described as a mystery of communion in faith, the sacraments (the signs of faith) and love (the incarnation of faith). Christ, the fullness of human experience, is this mystery of communion personally received in faith, made present in his all-powerful resurrection in the sacramental liturgy and, finally, lived out on all levels of our human condition through love in act.

In other words, the Church first of all *announces* the Christ-event. It is here at the point where faith is born that the gospel proclaimed by the whole Bible begins to become part of our experience. If it went no further, the Church would be nothing more than a Bible society and the Bible one more highly respected book amongst all of mankind's spiritual books. The Christian experience would simply be the imitation of a dead model and obedience to a rule of life. The gospel would be a dead letter. The individual would struggle with his search for balance and perfection. Historical and community solidarity would vanish.

But the gospel is "spirit and life" (Jn 6:63); it is a fact. Christ's pasch is not simply a memory but a present event. How is this so? It is here that the whole sacramental drama in which the risen Christ is both mystery and phenomenon becomes accessible to our senses while leading us beyond the appearances. The Bible, when it is proclaimed in the Church, announces Christ's pasch, but the sacramental liturgy makes it present, again actualizes it, brings it into the here and now. In the sacrament, Christ's pasch becomes contemporary to us and we become contemporary to it, now, in an existential way. The sacramental dimension of the Church of Christ is not of the same nature as the sacred rites which in other religions seek to reiterate an original mythical event.

It is an historical event, pregnant with the whole of history and making the present fruitful.

The Christian experience is liturgical not in an attempt to escape from time or to compensate for the absurdity of the present instant, but because it brings us into the fullness of the present instant. Through the liturgy the present becomes a step in the pasch of Christ, and we become actors in it. The fecundity of the sacramental experience reaches into every detail of our lives, making it possible to resolve everything in the light and the power of love.

The fact that the Christ-event is coextensive with the whole of human history opens us to the true dimensions of our Christian experience. It is the *experience of a presence*. Presence of God, of all men, of the whole of man. Presence of the world. From the very first spiritual achievements of *Homo sapiens* until now, all philosophies have set out to be the explanation and the salvation of man. If they have always left man unsatisfied—and that is equally true of a certain form of Christianity emptied of the experience of the living Christ— it is because one or another aspect of human experience has been neglected, inhibited or atrophied. Whatever that aspect may be, and the most important is death, the proposed way of salvation has always been developed within the realm of ideas. But man cannot be saved by ideas. He hungers for a presence. Only an experience of presence can bring him to fulfillment. Death and all its attendant disorder and waste, already present in our lives, cannot be exorcized by ideas. It must be lived and thereby brought within the realm of life and presence. This is the heart of the Christian passage:

everything irresistibly becomes life because everything becomes a living presence.

This event of a living presence is revealed in the Bible, made present in the liturgy and brought to fulfillment in the Christian life. It is the event of the living God and of man living in the mystery of Christ. Understandably, the New Testament, which introduces the essential novelty, describes the Christian experience in terms of power and of the Spirit. The paschal feast of Jesus is the celebration of the firstfruits. It is completed in the feast of Pentecost, which is the celebration of the harvest in which all men attain the fullness of life through regeneration in the Spirit. "Lift up your eyes and look at the fields, they are white with the promise of harvest" (Jn 4:35). The time we are now living is the time of the harvest, the time of the Spirit. It is in that same Spirit that the Bible must be read, for it is the revelation of the paschal mystery of the whole Christ from the sowing of the first seed to the gathering in of the last sheaf.

CHRIST AND THE UNITY OF THE BIBLE

The unity of the Bible lies in the mystery of Christ's pasch and our pasch in him. Very often the multiplicity of facts and thoughts that follow one after another in the books of the Bible is confusing to one who comes to it unaware. The result is either that one gives up the attempt to read it or that he is content to find some word of life here and there in it which corresponds to the need he feels and helps him to face up to his own life experience. Many Christians, even some with a long and solid religious formation grounded in Scripture, retain the impression that the Bible is complicated. The existential unity of it, which could bear fruit in their lives, has escaped them and they make do with a more or less scrupulous fidelity to certain principles and practices. In point of fact, the complexity lies in the reality of our human condition, but the Christian experience in itself is fundamentally simple. It all comes down to *living Christ*, Christ in the ever-present and personal power of his resurrection, Christ at work in the new humanity, the Church. The Christian experience is the experience of the "work of the Lord who is Spirit" (2 Cor 3:18). *It all comes down to loving.* In the following chapters the Christian experience will unfold in all its simplicity: Christ, love. God is love, and man has been created to live by love. All reality comes down to this.

The Bible should be read with an existential rather than a scholarly approach. God speaks in it through the men to whom he has entrusted the task of expressing him. Christ is the word of God made flesh. The Bible cannot bear any message for us other than that of Christ himself. It is very important to see things in this perspective, otherwise we may never really come face to face with Christ and with our own Christian experience.

For all practical purposes this means that we should read the Bible in the light of Christ who is, personally, the New Testament. Not that we should be satisfied to read only the books of the New Testament. On the contrary, we have to read them in the light of and with the aid of the Old Testament. If only for a purely literary reason one cannot fully comprehend the end of a literary work without putting it in the context of what has gone before. When Jesus speaks in parables or accomplishes a sign, he does so very simply, and yet every word and detail bring to the minds of those who see and hear him a whole context of understanding that they do not automatically bring to our minds unless we too are really nourished by the Old Testament. In a few words Our Lord could speak of the word of God as a seed or of his own mission as that of the Good Shepherd: for his contemporaries the images used by Isaiah, Jeremiah or Exodus immediately come to mind and give depth and meaning to Jesus' words. We shall never be so impregnated by the Old Testament that we can appreciate the slightest shades and tones of meaning in the New Testament.

But there is another reason, pertaining to the Bible itself and to its unity of divine authorship, which confirms that the New Testament should be read in the light of the Old. That is the overall design that runs through these two stages and makes them inseparable. A poor comparison would be to say that the Old Testament is like a dotted line which is filled in in the New Testament, or that the Old Testament is the map and the New Testament the land that it portrays. To understand the full design, we first have to look at the rough sketch. To find our way about an unknown country, the help of a map is often necessary. A constant reference to the Old Testament gives us a better grasp of the human fabric of the word made flesh and the phenomenon of the Bible takes on a greater consistence.

But the inverse is also necessary: the Old Testament should be read in the light of the New. In fact, this reciprocal movement is indispensable if one wishes to have access to the permanent message contained in the Bible. Christ himself initiated his disciples into a reading of Scripture in the light of his pasch (Lk 24). This is the reading in the Spirit by which the Spirit will guide us "into all truth" (Jn 16:3). Without this we might read the Bible as a human document of great religious importance but, nevertheless, as just a document. Without it we could go no further in knowing Christ than that first level of knowledge his contemporaries had and which Paul repudiates as knowing Christ "according to the flesh." An able biblical scholar could study the New Testament as a prolongation of the Old and could go far in his study, even without belief; he would nevertheless remain exterior to Christ. Not only intelligence but faith also must be at work if one is to discover Christ in the reading of the Old Testament. A reading in faith takes place, as it were, within the mystery of Christ. Christian tradition has called this a "spiritual" reading of Scripture. It is only possible if the reader is animated by the breath of the Spirit who gives life to the body of Christ.

That is why the Church, body of the risen Christ, can still use the words of the Psalms to express a Christian prayer. That is why the Old Testament texts used for the liturgy of the word in the sacraments are still able to convey the Christ-event that is made present in the sacraments. The Old Testament is fulfilled in Christ since it exists only in the function of Christ.

The method we shall use in the following chapters will, therefore, consist in reading the Old Testament in the light of the Spirit of Christ, knowing that an intelligent reading of it can bring much light to bear on the New Testament. In the first step we shall draw heavily on the contribution of the literary history of the biblical themes which unfold throughout the Bible from the time of preparation (Old Testament) to the time of fulfillment in Christ. But our attention will be concentrated primarily on the second step which will be to examine *in what way the Bible expresses Christ's—and hence our own—experience.* Both the Old and New Testaments will throw light on each other, and we shall see that the Old Testament is unified in this way. For it is the successive stages of the Old Testament story that reveal the dramatic dimensions concealed by the simplicity of the Christ-event. Thus although we shall reflect on the themes of creation, the promise, the pasch, exodus, the covenant, the kingdom, exile, the return to the Holy Land and the restoration, we shall not attempt to find an allegorical application of these major themes of the Old Testament to our present condition but rather try to find in them the internal structuring of Christ's pasch which is also ours.

One last remark should be made before we study the unfolding of the Christian pasch. With the coming of Jesus the "appointed time came" (Gal 4:4), all "was achieved" (Jn 19:28). The Old Law was "but shadows cast by future events, the reality is found in Christ" (Col 2:17). And yet that reality was nevertheless accomplished under the "veil of the flesh"; the full light of glory is reserved for the second and final coming of the kingdom. Are we, who live in the period lying between these two comings, to consider the events of Christ's life on earth also as shadows, as figures of a future reality? The answer we give this question will determine the significance of the events related in the Gospels and, in particular, the miracles. We find our answer in the risen Christ. If, to all intents and purposes, we eliminate the resurrection from the Christian experience, it becomes a purely moral experience, and the facts related in the Gospels can be given a moral interpretation just as can those of the Old Testament when seen as unrelated to Christ. This would mean that we were still in the time of shadows and figures. But if Christ is truly risen in the life of those who read the gospel, the facts of the gospel contain all reality for them, a reality that is so full of power that it cannot be limited to its initial enactment during the first thirty years of our era but is still and always present in its ontological fullness.

This brings us back to the sacramental reality which is inseparable from a spiritual reading of the Bible. If the facts of the gospel appear to pre-figure the realities of the future glorious coming of the Lord (Lk 20:14-18), it is because they make them present in advance under the veil of the sacramental mystery which is the mystery of Jesus' humanity, sacrament of the word and of his body, the sacramental Church of the present.

One can see the admirable unity produced by the event of Christ's pasch: the Old Testament is *illuminated* by it from within; the first coming of Jesus *makes it present* in reality, although under the veil of human mortality; the gift of the Spirit actualizes it ceaselessly in the body of the risen Christ, although still under the veil of the earthly condition of the Church and finally when the sacramental period has fulfilled its function of accomplishment, it will still be this same event that will *shine forth* in the light of Glory.

PART ONE

LIFE, THE UPSURGE OF LOVE

He who has been initiated into the hidden
power of the Resurrection knows for what
purpose God predisposed the beginning of all
things.

—Maximus the Confessor

CHAPTER ONE

Creation, the First Gratuitousness

THE BIBLE AND CREATION

Although the Bible, as we know it, opens with the poem of
creation, the first living experience of those men who began
to write the Scriptures was altogether different. The very first
experience which they attempt to relate and which bears
within itself the germ of all future developments is not a cosmic but a personal event. The primordial experience is not a
theory of the origin and development of the universe but the
event of the birth of a child which will command the future of
a people and of a land and, by progressive extension, the
development of all peoples and of the whole earth. That original event which introduces the first seed of the Bible is the
coming of the living God into the personal life of Abraham.
This eruption of life is not primarily of the biological or social
order; it touches a man in a yet unexplored and unsuspected
dimension of his being by initiating a dialogue between him
and someone who lives and of whom he was unaware.

Abraham, an anonymous member of one of the waves of Amorite migrants who swept over the Fertile Crescent at the beginning of the second millennium B.C., immersed as he is in his tribal value-system, yet experiences a new departure: an absolutely novel departure which uproots him from the rock of himself, as he knows it, and faces him with the invitation to walk with God and to attain fulfillment: "Walk in my presence and be perfect" (Gn 17:1).

Implicitly, of course, this departure reveals the God-Creator, but believers only developed a reflection upon creation much later when, strangely enough, the descendants of Abraham the Amorite returned temporarily to his native land, Chaldea. In spite of a tone which is fundamentally different, the similarity of literary style between the first chapters of Genesis and Babylonian writings is well known. The biblical view of creation is singularly illuminated for us by the very fact that until the time of the Babylonian Captivity all the attention was reserved for Abraham's descendants and the land they inhabited.

Men of Old Testament times did not elaborate a mythological, still less a scientific, theory of the creation of the world. They discovered the universe little by little, starting from the *dialogue with God* whom they knew, in the first instance, not as first cause or supreme being, creator of all things, but as the God who speaks and who communicates himself: I am your God. God is he who spoke to the Fathers and who continues to speak to his people. He speaks, not from afar, but as one who asks for a personal response, a personal commitment. When more highly developed intelligences began to speculate about creation, they quite naturally approached it from within the climate of dialogue. Hence we can understand the function of the creative word: it can be known as the origin of all things because it has, first of all, been experientially known as the origin of the people that has welcomed it and sought to give it a personal response. From the beginning, although implicitly, man's place in creation is a personal relationship to the living God: in him, through him, and for him, all things will be made coherent. The crowning point of the consciousness of this reality is reached in one of the most recent of the New Testament texts, the prologue of the fourth Gospel: "In the beginning was the Word.... Through him all things came to be...all that came to be had life in him" (Jn 1:1-4).

The presence of the Logos, the word of God at the origin of all things is not simply an initial putting into motion of creation or a first cause that can be rationally explained. It is a personal, living presence. Those who wrote about the creation could draw on several centuries of the covenant. Although the creation is seen as spontaneity on God's part, the first experience of that spontaneity was lived in Abraham's time, in the birth of the people born of his son.

We must try to understand from within the primitive religious mentality of the people of the Old Testament: constantly on guard against the degraded notions of the Godhead rife in contemporary pagan cosmogonies, they were led progressively to discover the fact of creation. And they discovered it in the fact of the birth of a child. Not simply in the physiological process which had always deeply impressed men of old, but, in particular, in the birth of that only child, Isaac. Isaac was truly the child of his parents, old though they were. He was also, in a very real sense, the child born of the word of God and of his promise. The experience of creation is thus centered both in man and in God's commitment to man. St. John's prologue, telling in sober terms the same story that Luke tells of the Annunciation, also contemplates the Word-Creator as the Word Made Flesh, totally man but born of God.

Thus creation is seen as an experience of a covenant. Already the God of the Old Testament is committed to his creation. He is not the God of philosophers who takes only a distant interest in a degraded product of his own perfection. He is the Father for whom creation is the act of calling other beings to union with himself. A centuries-long experience of the covenant was needed before Israel came to discover in man "the image and likeness of God" (Gn 1:26-27). And, with the recognition of this kinship—"for indeed we are his children" (Acts 17:28)—all that exists in the universe is seen to bear the imprint of God's features. In modern language we would say that the cosmic consciousness of the Bible is fundamentally personalist.

The term "cosmos" makes its appearance in the books of the Hellenist period (Wis 1:7; 2 Mc 7; 9; 23). It evokes the Greek concept of the order and beauty of a universe governed by the Logos. But the biblical context is far broader than that. In the perspective of the covenant the cosmos is no longer seen simply as a highly organized complex of pre-established laws into which man must fit with docility in order to come through the time of his earthly imprisonment with as little cost to himself as possible. On the contrary, it is seen as a state of chaos which gives way progressively to organization parallel to and alongside the progress of man himself (Gn 1:28). Just as, through the covenant, it can be seen that there is a destiny common to God and man so, little by little, the parallel development of God's people and of the world is seen to be in harmony. God, his people and the world live out the same drama (Gn 9:9-11).

Consciousness of this solidarity took shape only slowly. It began in the limited framework of the land inhabited by God's people. According to the conceptions of the ancient Eastern religions, a god was the owner, the baal, of a territory. To change territories was to change gods. The period of the Babylonian captivity was the occasion for Israel to make significant progress in the knowledge of God: beyond the borders of Palestine Yahweh is the Lord of all the earth, not just of the land given to the ancestors of the race.

After the return from exile, when it had become apparent that a radical transformation of that land was illusory, Israel looked to still wider horizons and recognized that the destiny reserved for the land was identical with the destiny of the whole earth. Its perfect humanization supposed a complete reversal of the irremediably chaotic universe in which we live. The way was thus opened to visions of new heavens and a new earth (Is 65:17; 66:22).

It is worth noting that this new awareness evident in the later writings of the Old Testament coincides with a keener perception of the origins of the race. This development is very revealing. It would be a misreading of the laws of human maturity to suppose that the writers of the books of the Bible began with the chronological beginning. They needed perspective, experience, maturity, and it is only toward the end of the Old Testament that the first dawning of the world can be perceived. At that moment a long passage has already been accomplished. But most important, the dawn of a new day is about to break: the day that is Christ. In the light that he sheds the first glimmerings of the world can be seen.

> He is the true likeness of the God we cannot see; his is that first birth which precedes every act of creation. Yes, in him all created things took their being...they were all created through him and in him; he takes precedency of all, and in him all subsist.... It was God's good pleasure to let all completeness dwell in him. (Col 1:15-19)

Every stroke and line of the biblical imagery depicting the creation converges in him: the word of God and his dialogue with man; the son in whose birth all life flowers; the covenant between God who is love and humanity, God's people; the likeness of God built into man's being which, in emerging, draws a humanized cosmos to God; the coming of the son, bringing with him the renewal of the whole universe; finally, the accomplishment of the world-order at the close of the immense human pasch.

CREATIVE EXPERIENCE

When the fact of creation is looked at in this perspective, what can we say of the "Christian experience" of this fact? "I will speak my mind in parables I will give utterance to things that have been kept secret from the beginning of the world" (Mt 13:25, quoting Psalm 78:2). He who understands Christ's cross and resurrection can understand the reason of every-thing and the end toward which all beginnings move.

There are two ways of knowing reality: from the out-side, as a measurable object, through observation and abstraction; this is the limitless field of science; from the inside, in a way which involves the knowing subject, by com-munion; this is existential experience which is also limitless. In what concerns a knowledge of the Bible there is, without a doubt, a preference for this second manner of knowing. The fact of creation is known, not systematically and analytically but according to a personal experience, from within. And this is also the way in which we must live it. When Jesus cures a paralytic on the Sabbath, he comes up against a formalism which contains the fossil of the poem of creation, and he makes the original meaning of the lesson it contains come alive again: "My Father has never ceased working and I too must be at work" (Jn 5:17). One cannot live the creation with-out entering into the movement of Christ's work. The verses that follow, in the same chapter of St. John's Gospel, show well enough where this work—which Jesus later compares to the pains of childbirth—leads to: the resurrection (Jn 5:21; 16:21). For one who is baptized, every day is a Sunday, the first day of creation and the day of the resurrection insepara-bly intertwined and seen as the Lord's Day, the "today" of God and of man in the risen Christ.

Creation is ours today for it is ceaselessly the begin-ning of the word in our lives and in the world. The first parable of creation is the parable of the sower (Mt 13): the word is the seed and we are the soil. His growth in us and ours in him contains such an abundance of possibilities that

31

neither science nor spiritual experience will ever exhaust
them. It contains all richness of being: cosmic, biological,
sociological, psychological, spiritual. Modern science, awakening from the euphoria of the discovery of the "Object," is
tending to reinstate man, as human subject, at the heart of all
theories of the cosmos. Science is simply coming back to the
first thrust of the word in the rhythm of creation. We have to
bring all our human potentialities to fulfillment within the
radius of that personal nucleus in which the whole of man is
brought to life: "All those who welcomed him he empowered
to become the children of God" (Jn 1:12).

However, if creation is always an experience of being
born to an abundance of possibilities, it is not, in the biblical
view, an absolute starting point: we are born of someone.
Creation is not just the baggage given to each one as he is
sent out on his journey—even if, some days, we feel that we
would like to set out again without baggage. It is dialogue
made possible. At our very origins it is the promised word
entrusted to us and woven into the very fabric of our being.
In other words creation in the Bible-view is not just a certain
number of risks that we have to run in order to reach the
goal: it is the goal itself gathered, and become interior to us,
in the form of our potentialities. If our personal fulfillment is
achieved in love, it is because that same love is not only at the
goal but also at the source. We are not only created at each
instant to love: we are first of all loved, and that is why we are
created. Love precedes and informs our personal becoming.
In this sense to experience creation is to experience the first
gratuitousness. Following on the act of creation, the whole of
the long drama of the human pasch in Christ will liberate our

potentialities for loving more and more. This is only so because at the source—and we ourselves are source in the measure that we are persons—is love. To love means to give oneself and to receive. Creation is the first act of our pasch: we exist because God gives himself. The working out of the drama consists in our receiving him and giving ourselves in a growing, personal liberty.

What took place in the literary composition of the biblical theme of creation takes place similarly in our lives. We only understand the beginnings in the light of fulfillment; we can only see how deep a valley is when we have reached a neighboring vantage point. For us, as for the people of the Bible, the experiences of our continual creation can become the experience of being loved. We need only a certain inner freedom which enables us to love in truth. But what are these fundamental potentialities of love, the hidden talents that the Father has entrusted to us to be developed (Mt 25:14-30)?

THE EXPERIENCE OF THE COSMOS

A superficial reading of the first chapters of Genesis can leave us with an image of the universe as nothing more than the scene in which the human drama is acted out. But if we read in an attempt to understand the mind of the authors and to discover the presence of Christ, the cosmos is seen to have quite another significance. The material world, which absorbs the greater part of human activity, is often banished as being foreign or even harmful to our spiritual experience. In Christ this dichotomy is unknown. In him there is not the "economic" man on the one hand and the spiritual man on the other. He "brings everything together" (Eph 1:10).

Modern man, victim of a truncated form of humanism, sees creation and the blind emergence of life almost exclusively as simply an object of science or as usable matter: it is all too rarely lived as an integral spiritual experience. One of the ways in which we do not keep faith with the risen Christ is this habit we have of shutting off our experience into separate compartments. In general the economic reality in our lives, our domestic or professional work, money matters, our food, clothing and housing, is rarely lived as fully part and parcel of the human and spiritual. Most people consider it to be a morally "neutral" sector of their active lives or even as incompatible with their deepest religious level of life. But the true Christian experience of the universe has no room for this vivisection and duplicity: it is unifying.

"If creation is full of expectancy, that is because it is waiting for the sons of God to be made known. Created nature has been condemned to frustration . . . with a hope to look forward to; namely, that nature in its turn will be set free from the tyranny of corruption, to share in the glorious freedom of God's sons. The whole of nature, as we know, groans in a common travail all the while" (Rom 8:19-22). The cook and the cosmonaut, the dressmaker and the engineer, the technician and the laborer can all live this exalting reality. The material world lives out the human drama in Christ: if we do not realize this the material world can dehumanize us.

In the light of Romans 8:19-22, of Colossians 1:15-19 and of the prologue of St. John's Gospel, we can reread the first pages of Genesis (chaps. 1–3). The first intention of the author is didactic: everything that exists, matter as well as man, is good with a fresh goodness because everything comes from a fullness of love and a life that gives of itself. At its source the experience of creation is "personal," illumined by the light of a countenance which attracts as it reveals itself: the whole of creation is "expectant," aspiring to the attainment of this countenance of light. And in the movement of creation toward God's beauty, man is not just one of the stones on the way: it is in him that God's countenance must emerge from darkness into light, and as he frees himself, progressively the whole of creation takes on the divine form.

The first chapter of Genesis is a poem, the second a love story, the third a drama. This literary form bears some relationship to the reality that it suggests. A poem cannot be reduced to a formal expression, it is a gestation, it is premonition and revelation of creation. For the God of love and light (1 Jn) creation is a poem in act. Its realism goes beyond the reach of literary endeavor, but, and this is far more wonderful, not beyond the reach of man's work. "My Father has never ceased working and I too must be at work" (Jn 5:17), and man works also in the same stream of creativity as the Father. The work of the incarnate word has been entrusted to man. Creation is not just a starting point in time, long ago; it is the movement that has its source in the Father and solicits our response in Christ at every minute of our lives. Our work can be very prosaic if it is kept in separate compartments but when it is integrated in Christ it becomes a creative poem. This is not just a beautiful theory: anyone who lives it has experienced the life-giving truth of it.

Every poem is a song. "Fill the earth and subdue it" (Gn 1:28). Whenever a man succeeds in raising himself above his work, his effort dilates his life and affords him joy.

But he must dig deep to the source of his joy or it will run dry. When we are in touch, within ourselves, with Christ at work then that joy becomes possible. For in him we are once again in touch with that original gratuitousness in which the material we work upon bears the fresh imprint of God, love giving itself. The Christian experience of work is an ever-new poem which, receiving its raw material as a gift of grace, by transforming it becomes, itself, a song of praise and gratitude. "Learn, too, to be grateful" (Col 3:15).

The second chapter of Genesis is a love story, the love story of man and the world. Here the literary form reveals a hidden realism. Man belongs to the earth. Paleontology and primitive symbolism sing the same refrain in their own ways: the earth is man's first maternal womb. When he lies on the ground or, as in certain funeral rites, in the ground, man often adopts the natural position of a fetus. The biblical account suggests two important elements amongst others: the original state of man is cognate to the earth; but the fact that the earth becomes habitable for man is, in itself, a free gift (the symbolism of the water which rises from the earth, Gn 2:4-7). If we do not reduce the fact of creation to a point of time in the past, our Christian experience of continuous creation can reach deeper levels.

The first level touches on the psychological dimension of our lives. An area that Jung called the "collective unconscious" and that Mircea Eliade has analyzed closely in the archetypes of different civilizations is rooted in man's experience of earth and the cosmos. The hidden potentialities of the unconscious seem to have their roots in the depths of our condition as a part of the cosmos. It would be too long to show here how, in this connection, the integral Christian experience in its biblical and sacramental, community and mystic dimensions is an experience of plentitude. For it contains all the possibilities stemming from man's earthly origins and, without denial or distortion, makes a reality of all the archetypes of the human condition: far from suffering them as a blind fate, the Christian experience frees the sap of life contained in them to bear new fruits of freedom and gratuitousness. There is a need today for an exegesis of the cosmic themes found in the Bible: earth, water, tree, rock, sun, space, time…which would show how all these archetypes are "personalized" in Christ and actualized in even the most spiritual dimensions of our personal lives through the efficacious symbolism of the sacraments. It is a fascinating aspect of our integral experience of the risen Christ.

If we go beyond the exquisitely sober literary shell of Genesis 2:4-7, we realize that the same gratuitousness is at work preparing the cradle, the body and the breath of life of man. The earth and the soul are born of the same love, and man, whose body comes from the earth, in turn gives life to the earth with the breath of life received from God. All of creation "is waiting for the sons of God to be made known" (Rom 8:19). Since the earth has not only brought forth man but has also been entrusted to man for its fulfillment, man must be more than simply a child of earth: he is also a child of God. Between the two poles of man's sonship a new gratuitousness comes into play, revealing God's first commitment in the cosmos for which man has received the responsibility. Verses eight and nine speak of the first plot of land entrusted to man

37

as a free gift. We have here the archetype of the garden: paradise.

We must be careful not to idealize this and fall into the rut of mythology. It is strikingly beautiful to see how, throughout the Bible, divine gratuitousness is often represented under the imagery of the earth. This confirms what we said earlier, that the experience of creation comes to the people of the Old Testament through the experience of the promise (child, land, nation) made to Abraham and which is slowly fulfilled in time in the history of Israel. The land is one of the objects of the promise. After the purification effected by the time of exile, far from the land of the fathers, and when the theme of "land" has been gradually extended to embrace the whole earth, domain of the living God, the New Testament leads to a new understanding of the nature of the land which is the inheritance of the patient and the poor in spirit and which is none other than the kingdom of heaven. The risen Christ is the plentitude of the kingdom and we, through the Spirit that is poured out on us, have become, communally and personally, the land filled with the Spirit of God (Is 11:9; Heb 2:14). This is how Jesus, when at the moment of his death he poured out his spirit over the whole of creation in an act of regeneration, could say to the good thief: This day you shall be with me in paradise (Lk 23:43). Paradise is the new humanity of which the risen Lord is the first born.

The paradise that Genesis speaks of is not, therefore, the mythical place of the golden age which survives in the nostalgic memories of all religions. We can only understand its authentic reality by reference to its true fulfillment: Christ.

Paradise is ahead of us rather than behind us. Or rather, since we know that it is already present in the crucified and risen Christ, it was already present, embryonically, at the beginning, just as earth and man existed in the beginning in the one, unique pasch of Christ. In the Christian perspective the first paradise is an expression of the initial gratuitousness in which man finds himself in relation to God and the cosmos.

From a literary point of view it must be noted that in these first two chapters of Genesis, the love story is older than the poem. The poem sings of man's vocation to govern and transform the world; the love story tells of the gratuitousness of the love that was at the origin of everything. Implicitly it paves the way for the crisis that is related in chapter three, for the human drama is going to be played out between the freedom offered to man and the freedom that he accepts, between the initial gratuitousness that brought forth man and the earth and the gratuitousness that man himself must achieve and which, while fulfilling man, will also fulfill the promises of the earth. The poem was written after the crisis: the love story gives only the preliminary elements. But both before and after the crisis man and the cosmos share a common destiny.

The Christian understanding of this seems to have survived better in the spiritual tradition of the East. At the present time, when Christians all over the world must find their own soul through a communion with the spirit of their fellows from other communities, an understanding of the cosmic meaning of the risen Christ is indispensable if we are to respond to the expectation of the modern, developing world which aspires, in a very real way, to that "revelation of the sons of God," that is, of living men. When modern scientists, technicians and "developers," who claim to be atheists because they have been unable to recognize in Christianity as it is lived a spirit that could give life to their aspirations, come to read and live what the early fathers sang of the cosmic pasch of Christ, then the Christian experience of creation will be a reality for the world in mutation.

What we stand most in need of today is to restore to the relationship between man and the universe, the initial impulse of gratuitousness that launched them in a vocation of solidarity. Because of the absence of this original gratuitousness the harmony that should govern their relationship is destroyed. On the level of matter the law can already be discerned: the harmony of beings rests upon the initial gratuitousness that brought them to be. Soon this law can be verified on the other basic levels of our existence: harmony between the flesh and the spirit, harmony in social relationships, harmony between man and woman, harmony in our psychological potentialities. But it is striking that things which are apparent to us in modern times are an explication of the intuitions of the Yahwist writers and of the second chapter of Genesis.

Today there seem to be two principal misconceptions concerning the divine gratuitousness that binds man and the universe in the same vocation: one which knows nothing of the Christian dimension of matter, in the manner of earlier humanisms, and the other which would dissolve man into the absolute of matter, in the manner of the utopian revolutionaries. Both in pure spiritualism and in pure materialism man and the humanization of the world are lost, whereas in reality man's vocation and that of the cosmos are bound in the same solidarity because the same gratuitous love has brought each of them into existence, and each for the other, on the road to the same personal goal of love. It is man who fulfills the world, but Christ who fulfills man. "It is all for you, and you for Christ, and Christ for God" (1 Cor 3:23).

However, all fulfillment must come about in accordance with the necessary laws of growth. To remain fixed in a universe not yet humanized would be to deny this fulfillment. Between the original, idyllic situation and the final humanization in Christ lies the time of the drama that must be acted out. This is the significance of the third chapter of Genesis. The harmony that is destined to reign between man and matter is not the product of the internal dialectic of the cosmos; the terrors of the atomic age are sufficient to dispel all such utopistic dreams of naturalism. The meaning of the drama in which we are engaged with the universe is that it is up to us to extract the seeds of gratuitousness that brought us and the world into existence, thereby actualizing it and transforming everything into gratuitous love, into God. Man's role in the world is to be its living conscience. It is not enough for him to be a conscious spectator who through science and empirical knowledge rediscovers the love that calls us into existence; he must also be a conscious participant and creator who frees the energies of all creation in order to personalize them in making them divine. "You will be as Gods" (Gn 3:5).

Herein lies the crux of the drama—and it is the same that has always existed from the first flowering of human

41

consciousness until today: are we going to accept the elements of our existence as a gift and, adopting a fundamentally self-giving attitude, bring them to their full realization? Or are we going to take possession of them, as surfeited and dissatisfied owners, and thus arrest them in their aspiration toward liberation? The sin that lies at the beginning (the original sin) is the type of all sin. It consists in opting for having rather than for being. Underlying it is a false notion of the gratuitousness of the origin and of the goal and, hence, a false notion of all that is real. The human drama is a becoming conscious but a becoming conscious of reality. In sin, on the contrary, there is an illusion, a seduction: man takes himself as absolute beginning and absolute end. In reality all that is, is a gift, a grace, whether it be the universe or ourselves. If we have a false conception of this, in the long run we shall have a false conception of the world, of ourselves and of God who is gift, gratuitousness, love. Everything springs from this free gift, and hence everything is made for a goal that lies beyond itself: the world will only be fulfilled in man, man can only be fulfilled in God.

In this connection a new theological intensity is apparent today. The sin of mankind is to choose false gods but, nowadays, the greasepaint of old idols has worn off. Modern consciences throw off the masks and uncover the true face of the perpetual, original crisis: man chooses to be his own god. We can all see concrete examples of this in everyday life and on the personal level. Choosing nothing but ourselves, we fall below ourselves, whereas when we choose to love, we choose God and thereby bring to fulfillment all the given elements of our existence whether in relation to our creative work, to others or to ourselves. This same drama is being played out by humanity as a whole and today more poignantly than ever before. It can be seen in the dramatic development of various human groups through the development of their material wealth. As long as men's choice is dictated by having, by possession rather than by true, human being, the economy will be radically corrupt, its disorder proclaiming the original sin of man who has allowed himself to be seduced by the lie of his self. To take just one example: a stable world price for primary products which can determine the economic and social development of newly independent countries has everything to do with the spiritual experience of the original drama of man: either man opts for possession of matter and makes himself his own god or, by choosing love, he opts for the liberation of matter.

The fact is that, on the whole, man has always chosen the first of these alternatives and one can understand St. Paul's affirmation: "Created nature has been condemned to frustration; not for some deliberate fault of its own, but for the sake of him who so condemned it" (Rom 8:20), that is to say: for the sake of man and his power to sin. We must therefore progress from a "vain" conscience to a true conscience—and that is our pasch. The original love story can only be fulfilled through a redressing of the situation which, in Christ, is called redemption. This will be the meaning revealed in the succeeding stages of biblical history seen as the stages of our own history.

It was necessary to see how, on the most material level of our existence, we are bound to the cosmos in a love story, a poem and a drama. The same "groaning," that of the Spirit is ours; the same "birth," that of the risen Christ is ours. Created nature is in a state of expectation. It is up to us to fulfill this expectation by becoming free with God's freedom. Creation is not a stage set for us. Through the Spirit it is the warp of our human fabric, and because of our sin it becomes in Christ the sacrament of our divinization.

CHAPTER TWO

Creation, Gratuitousness in Man

THE BODY EXPERIENCE

What we have just said about matter can be said even more emphatically about our own bodies, for they are our most intimate point of contact with the cosmos. And yet, as one of the primary elements of our experience, our body also has a meaning all its own. Starting from Christ, the perfect man, we can attempt to discern the meaning inherent in our own body-experience. Only Christ can show us the way that leads beyond the false dichotomies that are all too familiar to us, two of which, in particular, affect us, sometimes simultaneously.

On the one hand the modern attitude toward the body seems to be made up of unconditional trust which is probably a reaction to the exactly opposite attitude. And with this confidence and general lack of inhibition there goes an illusion of naturalism which sees man as simply a "thing" amongst many others and subject to the same, unavoidable laws. And so people refuse to recognize that there is any "problem" and, above all, reject all inhibiting "complexes." This attitude is encouraged by a pagan environment and propagated through the press, novels, movies, the all-pervading comfort of modern life, a loss of all sense of effort, etc.

On the other hand there is no firm moral sense, conscious or unconscious, even amongst the most "emancipated." Modern consciences seem to be ill at ease and affected by a diffuse sense of guilt, being governed by their notion of what is "allowed" and what is "forbidden." Here too the social environment is powerful: family training, group mores, a literalistic interpretation of religious laws…all this produces a collection of taboos, a vague Puritanism and a deep distrust of the flesh and particularly of sexuality.

In Christ the body-experience does not disregard the dual residue of history but assumes it realistically and in personal fulfillment. The Christian body-experience unifies all the elements of the human in line with the fulfillment of the cosmos: "From the beginning till now the entire creation, as we know, has been groaning in one great act of giving birth; and not only creation, but all of us who possess the first-fruits of the Spirit, we too groan inwardly as we wait for our bodies to be set free" (Rom 8:22-23).

Let us read in the light of Christ what Genesis has to say in 1:26-28 and 2:7. When God is described as fashioning man out of the dust of the earth, we are told that he breathes the spirit into him. This is the first expression of a truth that is going to recur constantly: when God creates a body, he creates it in his own image and imparts to it his own breath; he creates it in the image of his Son and through the breath of his Spirit. This is true of Adam and of Christ. It is true of the body of Christ, the Church, and of each one of us, his members. When the Father fashions the first man he models him after Christ, his own true image. And this is also true when our bodies take shape, for the Father works in an eternal "today" with us when he entrusts to us, as adults, the care of modeling ourselves. Born of love, our bodies are "waiting" to be fashioned in the likeness of Christ through the breath of the Spirit. And this is our work. We are still only rough sketches of ourselves.

> When it is sown it embodies the soul, when it is raised it embodies the spirit. If the soul has its own embodiment, so does the spirit have its own embodiment. The first man, Adam, as scripture says, became a living soul; but the last Adam (Christ) has become a life-giving spirit. That is, first the one with the soul, not the spirit, and after that, the one with the spirit. The first man, being from the earth, is earthly by nature; the second man is from heaven.... And we, who have been modeled on the earthly man, will be modeled on the heavenly man. (1 Cor 15:44-49)

The distinction made by the ancients between the body, the soul and the spirit has been adopted on the phenomenological level by modern psychology. Paul, however, has a more dynamic view: he sees man as a living being (the body animated by the life-principle: the *psyche*) and as a "spiritual" being (the whole man animated by the divine life: the *pneuma*) living in the Spirit. Our primitive condition, of the earth, is "psychic"; the soul is living. But our total condition, brought to fulfillment gratuitously by the Spirit of God from on high, is "spiritual": the Spirit gives life. We see here the movement from life-given to life-that-gives; from the biological that receives life to the spiritual that gives life.

And so, prior to any moral consideration is the fact that our bodies partake, in a privileged manner, in the humanization of the cosmos which is destined to be animated by the Spirit. For if the cosmos is the matter of the Spirit and the first gratuitousness of love, our bodies are, even more truly, the raw material of our spirit and the first flowering of our love. For just as the material universe is a resounding call to liberation of all spiritual potentialities, so our bodies are the first subjects to attain liberation from within. The cosmos is waiting to be transformed by man, to be humanized, personalized. Our own bodies are the first fruits in our work of transfiguration of the universe, the first summits of the biological order to partake not only of personal life but even of the divine condition.

This power of transfiguration which flows from the risen Christ through us orients our bodies to becoming more and more revealing of the deepest level of our being, to becoming more and more simply ourselves. At the same time it renders them capable of being a sacramental source for the transformation of the world. This is what our body receives when we communicate with the Body of Christ: "Didn't you realize that you were God's temple and that the spirit of God was living among you?" (1 Cor 3:16). The Spirit who has brought everything into existence and who is obscurely present on all levels of the cosmos, breaks out in luminous presence in the body of one who is baptized, transforming it into a sacrament of spiritual creation.

The mystery of Christ's transfiguration is ours. In the glory of Christ's body we can live the poem of our bodies and the love-idyll of gratuitousness between the Spirit and life. The principal biological functions stand in need of this breath of creation in order to reach their spiritual fulfillment. We must not forget that the spiritual is not in opposition to the corporeal but only to that way of bodily being that Paul calls psychic precisely because it is still a concealed life and not yet life which has become source. The life of the Spirit is not disembodied. It is life in which the flesh lives by the Spirit. In this dynamic experience some of our biological functions are seen to be transitory and relative, for example, the nourishment of life by eating which is seen as reaching fulfillment in the kingdom in the image of the banquet (Lk 22:16) and already anticipated in the sacrament of the body of Christ, or the function of reproduction, a process necessary to the preservation of the species and which reaches fulfillment in personal liberation (Mt 19:12; 22:30).

Some functions, on the other hand, are revealed as absolute and permanent: our body is the visible expression of our personal mystery. In the original gift of life nudity reveals not just "the flesh" but the person (Gn 2:25). It is the lie of sin that befouls it. Our conquest of ourselves must go far beyond a socially imposed modesty and reach an epiphany of simplicity: "When your eye is sound, your whole body too is filled with light; but when it is diseased your body too will be all darkness" (Lk 11:34). Our risen bodies will be the absolutely simple and transparent expression of the whole of our being.

Our bodies are also ourselves in communication with other personal subjects. As long as we remain immured in the murky depths of our possessiveness this is more a cause of separation than of union. But to the extent to which the Spirit we have received becomes active in us, our bodies are freed to become the dynamos of our knowledge of love of others. Here too the sacrament of the Body of Christ anticipates a communion of fellowship that knows no boundaries. "The fact that there is only one loaf means that, though there are many of us, we form a single body because we all have a share in this one loaf" (1 Cor 10:17).

The Christian body-experience is, therefore, the most deeply personal dimension of our experience of the cosmos and at the same time the most fully personal animation of the flesh by the Spirit. To reach this fullness, a pasch, a dying to the sin that darkens not our body but the heart is essential. Just as in the liberation of the cosmos, the creative experience of our body is redemption. From this flows the Christian attitude of simplicity and prudence, audacity and the full awareness of our weakness. This attitude transcends all moralistic conformity, for it is a mystical experience of the risen Christ. "You know, surely, that your bodies are members making up the body of Christ.... You are not your own property; you have been bought and paid for" (1 Cor 6:15, 20).

Our passage from the gratuitousness first given to us as a gift to that which has our own, personal assent carries the biological thrust present in the universe from the beginning of life through to fulfillment in eternal life, the life of love. While the first man's body is the fruit of the earth, the body of the risen Christ becomes the life-giving source of a new earth. But this paschal fulfillment is not the result of some inevitable sequence of events. It is the fruit of a reversal, or rather a new beginning, of creation in which the summit becomes the foundation. It is the irruption of life, in person, into our earthly condition. Already we have a part in this twofold condition: psychic and spiritual, Adamic and Christic. Our own fulfillment will also be the fruit of our passage through death which can now be seen, not as a failing of momentum, but as the last threshold that we must cross.

> When this perishable nature has put on imperishability, and when this mortal nature has put on immortality, then the words of scripture will come true: Death is swallowed up in victory. Death, where is your victory?... So let us thank God for giving us the victory through our Lord Jesus Christ. (1 Cor 15:54-57)

THE EXPERIENCE OF RELATIONS

Through its roots in the cosmos and the inherent attraction turning it toward the spirit, our body makes of each one of us a being standing in relation to all other human beings both on the biological and on the spiritual level. This relation is experienced by us as ambivalent. Another human being with whom we begin to communicate becomes close to us, but before this closeness can become the "neighborliness" of the gospel and a relationship of communion, a new pasch must be enacted. The "other" can be felt as both bitter and sweet, as a pole toward which we are drawn by a deep-seated need and as a being to whom it is well-nigh impossible to become attuned. Others both attract and repel us.

And so a relationship with another human being is a new experience of creation in which we recognize the basic theme but in which we see additional exigencies. It is an offer of gratuitousness that can only come to fruition in a gratuitous acceptance. The axis of growth of a relationship passes through our emotions, and both our own experience and the findings of psychology go to convince us that we are emotionally mature to the extent to which we can accept and welcome another just as he is, without being dominating or possessive. Another can be the object of our desire, but if he remains simply an object for our use not only is he wrongly appreciated but we, ourselves, are the first to be hurt. If, on the other hand, through an ongoing paschal movement the other becomes a free subject known and loved for himself, then together we can reach a harmonious relationship that can be creative for both. Man can only really possess what he has already given away. This is the first beatitude (Mt 5:3), law of the new creation already inherent to the first creation. No relationship with another human being can exist without love, and no love can exist without a spirit of giving.

Biblical reflection on this theme is developed in a very interesting way. In the accounts of creation that touch on the social fact contained in chapters one to eleven of Genesis, a reflection develops from an actual experience and works back in time, retracing the steps of a centuries-old experience of the covenant, an experience of love. It is this experience that has been lived by the descendants of Abraham that is found in the first human couple. At the other extreme, in the future, it will culminate at the resurrection in the covenant between Christ and his Church.

In this saga we can recognize our own path of development. Our present feelings for others are conditioned by what they have been for us and we for them during our early years. Our childhood experience in the family is the basic fact, a fact of creation, from which our social personality has developed. But however revealing it may be to look into our past and see our relations with our parents, this can only be liberating to the extent to which it enables us to go out of ourselves and accept them in the present with lucidity and in self-giving. This is the pattern of Christ's relationship with all human beings, and it is his self-giving that transforms them into a new humanity, the Church.

The unfolding of biblical revelation could be compared to an analysis in depth of the human community which makes us conscious of our origins and restores us, in the liberation of Christ, to the fecundity of the present moment. The poem, the love story and the drama must be taken as a whole which concerns us here and now.

The poem of creation sings of man as the personal appearance of the image of God in the world of life. Man is not called "the image" of God—this expression is reserved for Christ (Col 1:15)—it is said that he is made "in the image" of God as though this expressed a potentiality which, although real, has still to be actualized in conformity with Christ (Rom 8:29). Man is in the image of God because he is a mystery of personal communion: "God created man in the image of himself, in the image of God he created him, male and female he created them" (Gn 1:27). Man's reality therefore is not that of an isolated entity, a solitude that has received form, but of a capacity for communion, an "openness to." He becomes himself only when he becomes communion with another.

The human fact seen as the experience of relations is thus an integral component of the mystery of man and woman, incarnation of God's mystery. The deepest level of the human phenomenon is not reproduced, as a carbon copy, in exactly the same way in a man and in a woman, as if the sexual differentiation was ordered only to the biological end of the preservation of the species. By the Spirit who enters into the biological reality, and by the fact that man attains the level of personality marked with the imprint of the divine reality, a human being is a "being toward" the other. Just as in the Trinity the reality of each person is to "be toward" the other in a unique communion which is unity, so, in man, the human person only attains fulfillment in a paschal movement toward union with others. From the depths of God-Love springs an eternal mystery of relation, of giving and receiving. This is the mystery that brings man into being in the likeness of God and makes him man and woman with a capacity for loving. Finally this same mystery culminates in Christ: in him all creation reaches its climax because his fullness is the Church (Eph 1:23) in which all humanity, born of the first woman, reaches its apotheosis. In Christ, Jesus and the Church are one, not in an impersonal fusing of identities, but in the fullness of a personal communion.

Paul invites us to recognize this union between Christ and his Church in the idyllic account of Adam's union with his wife in Genesis (Eph 5:21-33; Gn 2:18-25). The

Yahwist text has one immediate lesson: the unity and stability of marriage (Gn 2:24; Mt 19:5-6). But its message does not end there. It is striking that a human relationship that is destined to reach fulfillment in Christ is here envisaged in the context of marriage and the family. The family appears as the type of interpersonal relations. And this first impression is confirmed if we follow the development of the biblical notion of "neighbor." At first a man's neighbor is always seen as one to whom he is bound by blood relationship and, later, as a member of the tribe or nation. It is only after the coming of Christ's Spirit that fellowship is seen to extend to all men and that the bonds of flesh and blood give way to a recognition of the bonds of the Spirit and of love. But the original type has lost none of its essential significance. The Bible reveals the drama of our relations with others through the example of the family relationship because the quality of the interpersonal relations in any society will be a reflection of the quality of its marriages.

This approach to the whole topic of "man in relation"—by a picture of the hard-won union of man and woman—has the advantage of placing the individual persons in a realistic light that brings out to the full the radical "otherness" of their deep, mutual attraction and the fullest expression of communion. The man-woman relationship is the prototype of all human relationships and embraces all the positive and all the negative values of other relationships. It can be said to contain the maximum of determining elements while demanding the optimum personal liberation. This description of a type of the human couple that we find in the very first pages of the Bible is all the more noteworthy in that it was written at a time of burgeoning spiritual maturity, fruit of the Babylonian Captivity (c. sixth century) and the preaching of the prophets. The sense of personal responsibility was growing in line with a sense of community solidarity and was just beginning to free itself from a conception in which the individual and the group were one and subject to the same ethical-biological imperatives. In the idyll of chapter two of Genesis we see the first expression of this growing awareness, and when one compares it with some of the notions that prevail in so-called enlightened societies today and the socio-biological imperatives that weigh on many modern marriages, one realizes that this old, sixth-century Bible story reveals a very progressive outlook.

Adam needs a companion, a partner in encounter (Gn 2:18). But, although it is not good for man to be alone, he cannot be satisfied with just any presence. He needs a living countenance not just a living being. He is dissatisfied with the animals (Gn 2:19-20), and yet, as we see in the scene where he names the animals, he continues to entertain the illusion of being able to fulfill himself in a solitary domination and transformation of the world. In the ancient East to name someone or something was to assert one's power over a being. But man does not need power alone. He also needs to encounter a being who is both the same and different from himself and with whom he can enter into dialogue. He needs a partner who will reflect his own being and, at the same time, draw him out beyond the limits of his self. A real relationship with another is from the start built on gratuitousness, and this is the deepest yearning of personal beings.

The symbolism of Adam's rib—in spite of its numerous literary antecedents in the East—still contains new treas-
ures of spiritual understanding. It suggests the mystery of
knowledge which runs like a thread through the whole biblical drama: to know another is to be born of him, to be born
with and to him. This idea is especially clear in the nuptial
theme that the prophets used to describe the relationship
between Yahweh and his people. A man and a woman are
born of each other and to each other in love because it is the
Father's love that has been entrusted to them and that must
bear fruit in marriage. This is why they are *one*, both flowing
from the same, free source. The Christian too is one with
Christ, springing from the open wound in his side (Jn 19:34).
But a man and a woman are also totally *other* and are, thereby,
in a position to communicate, to *become one*, each by the giving of his personal mystery and the receiving of the mystery
of the other. In the same way God and man, and each man
with all others, can become one in the same pattern of giving
and receiving. This is the communion of Christ and his
Church that is brought about in our midst. The pasch of our
relations with others is lived out in the tension between these
two gratuitous gestures of giving and receiving.

But this pasch has dramatic dimensions, and chapters three to eleven of Genesis give us due warning. It is not
an idyllic fatality that causes a human being to be born of
another and be born to him. Since the key to the whole drama
is gratuitousness, a crisis of free choice is necessarily
involved. There can be no love without it. In marriage, just as
in all interpersonal relations, there must be a maturing.
Genesis 2:24 suggests one stage in this maturing when it

says: "This is why a man leaves his father and mother and joins himself to his wife, and they become one body." The psychological perspicacity underlying this passage is quite striking when one has seen the results of emotional immaturity in adults. Someone who is really an adult is capable of relating harmoniously to others in society, but to reach this maturity one has to go beyond a stage of emotional adolescence. The first step in this process is to accept to be "other" than those from whom one has received everything in life and life itself. But the crux of the drama lies in the testing of gratuitousness portrayed in the story of the Fall (Gn 3). Anyone who knows something about life knows that when he chooses gratuitousness he opens the door to an expansion of being and to joy. But logically, if this is the vital environment of every personal being, it cannot remain a pure abstraction. No abstraction has ever nourished a man. In the Genesis account the crucial test of the human condition is presented straightforwardly and realistically. If we choose gratuitousness, we are not choosing an idea or even a value. We are choosing someone. Man, the dwelling-place of the Spirit, can only waste away if he tries to subsist on the infraspiritual realities. The original testing of love is when man is faced with the choice of accepting or refusing gratuitousness, of accepting or refusing the living, personal God who is the perfection of personal gratuitousness because he is love.

When we mentioned, in speaking of the cosmos, that man's sin lay in choosing the infraspiritual as an absolute, in choosing himself in his "psychic" condition, we saw that this entailed a dissolution of all consistency both in himself and in the cosmos—both became lost in the same aimlessness. On the level of personal relations we are faced with exactly the same challenge: either we choose gratuitousness and reach out to God and man in the indissoluble bond of the same love, or we choose our possessive self and divisiveness is enthroned in our hearts, cutting us off from both God and men. From the first awakening of man's emotional life, everything has a meaning in relation to Christ, in relation to love incarnate. Genesis 3 illustrates how egoism causes both the light of man's own countenance and the light of God's presence in him to decline and fail. As soon as they choose their own solitary selves, the man and the woman are divided and the reflection of God-Love is tarnished in them. They are deprived of the glory of God (Rom 3:24). The emptiness that seems to cloy so many human contacts surely stems from this.

Chapters four to eleven of Genesis reveal the disastrous sequence of events that flow from this first refusal of gratuitousness. Love should have been the vital medium of human beings. As soon as it is banished, egoistical sin guards the entrance to man's heart (Gn 4:7) and man becomes "angry and downcast" (Gn 4:6). Assassination and death reign in place of the unfolding of life: "For the wage paid by sin is death" (Rom 6:23); "if you refuse to love, you must remain dead; to hate your brother is to be a murderer, and murderers, as you know, do not have eternal life in them" (1 Jn 3:15).

Human fellowship cannot be founded only on the fact that we have the same origin; this would limit us to the purely biological level. Human fellowship must be freely chosen if it is to become a true community solidarity. Cain's fratricide is the prototype of this inverted caricature of human relations, and his descendants continue and accelerate the rot until it ends in the final disruption of Babal. The symbolism of the Tower—borrowed from the Babylonian Temple-towers—continues the teaching of the story of original sin: in setting himself apart from God, man set himself apart from his fellow-men. When he chooses himself as his own god, he deprives himself of all communion with his fellows by depriving himself of the glory of God; proof by negation and by the absurd of the unicity of love in which God and man, source and manifestation of the same light, share a common destiny. Only at Pentecost, when the risen Christ pours out the fullness of his Spirit on man, will he be restored to his vocation to love and to reflect God's radiant glory in his own clear countenance.

But the world, even though corrupt and deprived of love, bears within itself a solidarity which will prepare the way for its own redemption. During the laborious upward haul by which the species strive to reach perfection in the person, the individual in a personal communion and the collectivity in the community, a twofold solidarity is stubbornly affirmed: a solidarity in the extension of time and in the density of the present moment. Every ideology that has ever held sway on this earth has held and taught this truth: all men are bound to the past, bearing within them the heritage of their forebears and, whether fruitfully or in degeneracy, we are the offspring of a culture. This linear, historical solidarity is operative, whether we like it or not, on the level of the human nature which is our first endowment. Christian tradition situates the transmission of original sin within this order. We are

born deprived of God's glory, deprived of personal gratuitousness simply as the natural consequence of our human
solidarity.

However, we soon take this situation upon ourselves
by taking position, personally, in the same way as the first
couple. For them sin was personal and original. For us, *our
own sin* is also personal. And it is here that we encounter the
other aspect of human solidarity which is no longer simply on
the level of nature but on the level of the person. In the present moment, in the depths of our being and in the mysterious
interaction of consciousness, our personal responsibility is
engaged in regard to the whole of man. The original question
is the same, today, for every sinful man: "Where is your
brother?" And the answer we usually make is still the same:
"Am I my brother's guardian?" (Gn 4:9). Of itself, both on the
personal level and on the level of nature, man's twofold solidarity operates in favor of death and the egoistical refusal of
love. It must be assumed by Christ before this movement can
be reversed and it can be free to function in favor of life and
the community of love. Christ is the Son of God who assumed
"the condition of a slave" (Phil 2:7) and bore our faults in his
own body (1 Pt 2:24). The personal gratuitousness that can,
at last, exist and flourish in the human family lies in him. This
is why the early Fathers of the Church called God's Plan of
redemption for the world a plan of "recirculation" or "reinte-
gration." And this plan is set in motion from the moment
of the first refusal by the first human couple and stamps
the whole of human history with the seal of God's patience
(2 Pt 3:9). The dialectic of man's egoistical refusal and
God's loving gratuitousness comes into play from the very

beginning of Genesis (3:14-19), and from the beginning it involves the pedagogy of the promise which we shall see is the first stage of our human pasch.

God is faithful. Man, created in God's likeness, is a call to a personal relationship, a vocation to communion. He is, necessarily, free in the face of this vocation; to fulfill it must be his own choice since that vocation is the highest form of gratuitousness. God is faithful. The cosmic covenant revealed in the story of Noah (Gn 6:9) is already a sign of God's fidelity in his relationships. "I am now as I was in the days of Noah...for the mountains may depart, the hills be shaken, but my love for you will never leave you and my covenant of peace with you will never be shaken" (Is 54:9-10). Jesus is to be the personal "yes," fulfilling all the promises of that tremendous love that never lets itself be discouraged by our meanness (2 Cor 1:20). He gathers up the loose threads of history; he restores to the face of every human being the light of true brotherliness no longer as a disembodied ideal but in the reality of our disillusionments. In the risen Lord and in the crucifying experience of the cross which says "yes" to all gratuitousness and unties the knots of our refusal our twofold solidarity can, at last, lead us to life: "If it is certain that through one man's fall so many died, it is even more certain that divine grace, coming through the one man, Jesus Christ, came to so many as an abundant free gift" (Rom 5:15).

SELF-EXPERIENCE

Man already lives an experience of self on those levels we have just spoken of as being the primary given elements of his existence: the cosmos, the life of the body and his relation to others. So, if we now look at the purely personal experience, it must be clear that it is not because it is isolated from what has gone before but simply in order to better discern the originality of its own axis of growth. And, as in the previous points, the first thing that strikes us is that our personal experience is complex.

When seen from within, the richness of our being unfolds on an ascending scale. Our automatic reflexes reveal our oneness with the world of physics, whereas the natural impulses and energies constantly coming to the surface reveal that we belong to the world of biology. Above and beyond this, the outline of our personality begins to take shape under the formative influence of our social environment. In the gradual emergence of our conscious self we learn to distinguish and judge our different situations and states of mind, and we find that, even deeper within us, a whole world which we cannot lay hold of troubles and orients us in a disconcerting variety of ways. Even when we claim to master our actions and direct them in line with our conscious norms and values, we often have a lurking suspicion that we are really no more than puppets of our environment rigged out in the ludicrous garb of our own unconscious.

One can understand how so many first-class minds, seeking a clear-cut view of reality, have attempted to escape from the maelstrom by the path of positivism, considering man as only one, amongst other, measurable objects that can be scientifically classified. But this, precisely, is the illusion we must guard against. If we only consider man from the outside, as an object, we deprive him of that which makes him specifically human. Why is it that the positivists have such a repugnance for turning the searchlight of their much-vaunted consciousness, which sweeps over all reality, onto and into themselves? Does not the world of subjects belong to the real world that can be known? One of the most scandalous deficiencies of modern science is that, until very recent years, the knowing subject was banished from the field of knowledge. Depth psychology—to quote only one example which is not immediately suspect as metaphysical obscurantism—earns no respect in Marxist materialism: it smacks too dangerously of an inner world and of the person.

But the human maelstrom remains our basic question. However much light we may bring to bear upon the different levels of our personality already mentioned, from the purely mechanical to the ethical, we shall nevertheless remain divided and in a state of tension. Our constant, personal question remains: *how can we reach inner balance?* This question arises not from any one of the different lines of force of our being but from their highest point of convergence, and, similarly, it will only find an answer at this point of convergence, for it is only possible to reach interior unity on the highest level of our being. At this point each one of us can become our true selves; the point of convergence of all our different life-currents is the spiritual locus of our self-experience.

The biblical elements in this regard are soberly presented and unpretentious, although those already indicated concerning the cosmos, the body and human society culminate here, giving rise to the unfolding of the paschal drama of man. All of reality converges on this level. The poem of creation reveals the point at which man reaches his synthesis when it sings of the Spirit taking possession of him: man is made in God's likeness (Gn 1:26-27). The human condition, as such, is to live divinely. Man's unity has to be achieved, chosen, because his pole of unification lies within and is superior to himself. It is gratuitous. Experience proclaims that man is on a journey. The biblical poem murmurs that man is a vocation, a call.

The love story of chapter two speaks of the gratuitousness that originates the human vocation. We have already seen that the theme of water in the Bible symbolizes the free-flowing Spirit (Gn 2:5-10; Rv 22:1-2:17). The theme of the Tree of Life embellishes and adds detail to the symbolism. Man is seen as the last comer in the unfolding of life because in man the "psychic" is fecundated by the spiritual, feeling by consciousness and instinct by giving. This means that the new life which is necessary for him to be himself must, nevertheless, be the object of his own free choice. We keep coming back to the first paradox of the human condition: we are made for the gratuitous, but if it is imposed upon us it is no longer gratuitous. The novelty of man, as he appears on the Tree of Life, is that his life is lived in consciousness, in the Spirit and in love. Love can offer itself but can never be imposed. An understanding of this is fundamental. Without it one can understand nothing about man or about Christ, one can know nothing of God. Man has sprung forth, by a personal gift of the living God, as the highest branch on the tree of life, but because his life-blood is gratuitousness, he himself has to choose to be the fruit of the tree.

The dramatic testing of man is told in chapter three and it turns upon this truth and this first temptation: love, like joy, is not a fruit that one plucks for one's own enjoyment, but one that can only be had by giving. Man cannot fulfill himself and "become God" by plucking a fruit exterior to himself. In so doing he simply debases himself to the level of the object of his desire. He only fulfills himself, becomes as God, when he *is* the fruit, when he gives himself. We become ourselves in the giving of ourselves. This is the pinnacle of maturity at which the tree of life bears its wondrously human fruit. We are not only children of the earth, we are also children of God. We are not only "psychic," we are also spiritual beings. In order to reach fulfillment, man has to choose freely and to accomplish his divine condition. We are modeled after God, in his likeness, as soon as we take on the form of a gift, an offering of love. The first man and we who come after him are well on the path to maturity. The new man, Christ, is the fruit that has reached maturing on the true tree of life: the Cross.

EXPERIENCE OF GOD

The experience of creation is, at every instant, a revelation of God. But it is not only that, it is also his gift of himself. The positivist aberration that blinds us to the true identity of man also gives us a totally distorted image of God. As though God could be known from afar, coldly and objectively, without dramatic involvement! A sincere self-experience plunges us necessarily into an experience of this unknown God. "Anyone who fails to love can never have known God" (1 Jn 4:8). If we wish to reach him, we have to consent honestly to return to the well-springs of our own being. It is in the very act of responding to the thrust of gratuitousness within us that causes us to exist (*ex-sistere*—to stand out to) that we shall begin to recognize God as a "subject" who also "stands out" to us. He weaves himself into our lives and becomes, with us, the fruit of love.

At each moment in our lives gratuitousness beckons to us, and at each moment we can accept or reject it. Freedom is an experience, not a metaphysical possibility. It comes from God and is offered to us, never forced on us. At the beginning, as now, what is at stake is whether we shall choose to be a source and not simply a recipient of life. We are offered the choice between being a child of the earth, with a distorted relationship with the cosmos, life itself and other persons, or being a child of God capable of establishing ourselves in a harmonious relationship with all levels of being as we allow the original free gift of grace to grow and bear fruit in us and through us.

The Bible is more than just a book; it is alive with the presence of God. It is a melody that echoes within our hearts, a poem that our daily lives re-create. Very often our congenital tendency to rationalize dries up the springs of poetry within us . . . who could possibly feel emotion for a "first cause" blindly ruling the universe from afar? But the Bible reminds us that God is not the god of philosophy, he is the Creator because he is the birth of all things. When humanity had been prepared by God's long patience to give welcome to the true fruit of the Tree of Life, he came in person and took upon himself the total human condition, with the exception of sin, by being born as a man. The birth of the word in human flesh is the dawn of that new creation that will reach its apotheosis in the resurrection.

If God is birth, man is a being reborn in him. To be reborn of the Spirit as the body of the risen Christ is to be reborn to true love in the heart of God and of men. But a rebirth, through the dark night of death and sin that enfolds us, is more than the first awakening to gratuitousness of the dawn of creation. It is a veritable resurrection, a return from death.

All the new beginnings of our experience of creation converge in Christ's resurrection. Everything is drawn together along the axis of the Cross reaching out toward life and love. We caught a glimpse of this when we discussed the fundamental elements of the human condition: the cosmic reality, the biological reality of our bodies, the solidarity that binds us in the community of men and the interiority of our personal drama. And in the risen Lord we have recognized the basic law of creation: the harmony we are striving for is attainable only on condition that we recognize and put into practice in our lives the free gift of love that is the root and foundation of all harmony in the universe.

This primordial experience of creation is, in the risen Christ, the experience of the whole of humanity. It is the emergence of the Church, the presence of Christ's fullness, in spite of the petty human weaknesses that disguise it. For the Church is the tension of the first creation striving, in Christ, toward the new creation. The theme of the passage from chaos to cosmos through the action of the word and the Spirit of God is simply the original biblical theme: it is the leit-motif of our lives as men. It is the Church, the pasch of creation, and it lies within our grasp.

But the cosmic pasch is not the easy and inevitable fruit of a smooth, effortless process of liberation. It is a drama in which the primary force is a personal intervention, a gratuitousness. The smooth flow of events is disrupted by the play of two poles of freedom: God's free gift and man's free response. The pasch follows from and is acted out between these two poles of love.

PART TWO

THE UNFOLDING OF LIFE

The soul goes through many stages. At each stage it is flooded with the light of Wisdom and it will come, at last, to the Father of all light.

—Origen

CHAPTER THREE

The Promise, the Awakening of Freedom

"We have come here to tell you the Good News. It was to our ancestors that God made the promise but it is to us, their children, that he has fulfilled it, by raising Jesus from the dead" (Acts 13:32). Our first experience of creation leads to total resurrection in Christ, but when it is first offered to us it is in the form of a promise. Why does our pasch begin in this way?

The awareness of God's plan was born and grew, in the Old Testament, from the starting point of the promise made to the Patriarchs and their descendants. The prime era of the promise was the time of Abraham, Isaac and Jacob, but with the unfolding of events it becomes more precise as time goes on. The signposts that guide us on the path of our Christian experience are the successive promises, reaching nearer and nearer to fulfillment: *Moses* and the themes of the pasch, Exodus and the covenant; *David* and the kingdom, the *Prophets* and the exile, the return and the restoration; the first coming of *Christ* and the inception of the eternal Liturgy. Ever since Abraham—and even before, when man made his first choice (Gn 3:15)—humanity has lived with a promise. This promise is more than just a moment of the past that was lived in the days of the Patriarchs. It is an integral part of today's history also.

Why is this? To live with a promise is to live, as it were, with a seed, and life is a continuous progression and new growth. When we say that the resurrection is the fruit of the promise, we are also saying that the fullness for which we are created has not been forced upon us as a finished product from the beginning but has been offered to us as the fruit that will come out of our efforts and as a progressive liberation to which God commits himself with us. To promise is both to offer, or "put before" and to commit oneself, or "set oneself to" something. Each one of us is a promise of life, moving forward in expectation of the harvest. Our true youth lies ahead of us on condition that we truly commit ourselves with God.

Could it not be that the doubt and sterility that mark so much of our experience come from our ignorance of this fundamental law of life? A force of inertia and lethargy lies deep down in all of us. The "psychic" man expresses this when he wishes he was born as a finished product, set on the tracks that have to be followed, with no suffering, no problems, no questions asked. We seem to have a sort of nostalgia to be inanimate things, a regressive wish that slows down the impetus of our personal becoming. But we have been launched into existence precisely in order to become what we are. The promise is God's way of teaching us to *become*.

The promise indicates that God intends to teach us freedom. If freedom were forced on us, we would be no better than material things. What is more degrading than a devotedness that forces itself and its gifts on the recipients with no concern for their wishes and allowing them to share in the giving? This is precisely how a child is spoilt and becomes a spineless adult. Even if we are created for the divine condition, God is not going to stuff his adoption down our throats: he offers it to us and gives himself to us only in accordance with our response. The promise is God's way of teaching us on the level of the Spirit. A gift that was not initially a promise could deprive us of all human greatness by treating us as things. But, made in God's likeness, we can only find fulfillment in gratuitousness. All the inherent potentialities of creation must take the path of the promise in order to bear fruit for eternity.

THE PROMISE: AN INVITATION AND A GIFT

Our God is the Living God and He speaks to us.

It is true that everything that exists is an expression of the word of life. In the beginning of all things, always, is the Word (Jn 1:1; Gn 1:1-15), and if we exist it is because we have been called into existence by that living and loving word. But this does not mean that the experience of reality necessarily leads us to the discovery of the Living Being that has set all reality in motion. In history, the encounter between man and the word of God has never followed a logical, ascending curve (Rom 1:19-22) for the Living God is not to be found as the conclusion of syllogism. The encounter has never been touched off on the level of things but only on the level of the gratuitous presence that they conceal. No one can be known by another unless he consents to reveal himself, and he can do this only by a free act, in love. If this is true for us—as it is—could it be less true for God?

When God breaks into Abraham's life, he does so in a free and personal act. It is the beginning of a *dialogue*. When a man encounters God for the first time, he cannot refuse to take a stand that reveals himself. For, when God reveals himself to us, he also reveals us to ourselves. This is the nature of every dialogue in which the partners—on condition that they really listen to each other—begin to exist for each other. God began to exist personally for Abraham and Abraham for God from the moment of their first dialogue. But God's way of speaking to us is very different from so many of our discussions. God does not make himself known verbally. When he "speaks," he gives himself in his word and, in the most existential sense, he gives his word. His word is his son. And so God's gift to Abraham is a son, figure of the incarnate son in which he will give himself totally. In this unique dialogue everything becomes a gift, on both sides: Isaac is the son of the promise and of Abraham just as Jesus is the son of God and of Mary. The promise, then, is a gift on the level of the person.

"Have no fear, Abram" (Gn 5:1). Most of the events in which God reveals himself and which mark the unfolding of the promise in both the Old and New Testaments begin with two characteristic signs: a *name* and a message of *peace*. This is very different from the dreadful manifestations of the sacred that are the projections of human imagination. When the Lord intervenes in our lives he calls us by our name, which is more than the conventional label that is socially useful. It denotes the deepest, most authentic self, still only a misty outline, waiting to be brought into sharp focus through the knowledge and love of another person. We know all about having a "good name" or "making a name" for ourselves in society. But we also know that, on the level of our personal and emotional fulfillment, we only truly exist when we exist for someone. In a case of great distress what is more destructive than to be ignored, to be unwanted by anyone? And, equally, how do we behave toward someone we want to exclude from our lives? We cease to talk to him. But God, reaching out to us from within ourselves, calls us by our name. His pure interiority enters into communion with our still complex interiority. Often, just as we are ignorant of our true "calling" or vocation, we are ignorant of our true name, and God tells us: "Do not be afraid…I have called you by your name, you are mine" (Is 43:1-4). In the same movement of recognizing our calling, we hear our name and we recognize him who calls us to his love.

But we cannot help but experience the invasion of our private life by someone else as a threat. When we listen to someone else, in a dialogue, we can often discern a defensive movement within us to the extent to which we allow the other to penetrate our inner self. We hesitate to commit ourselves, wondering whether the presence that is offered will be one that will enslave us or free us, whether it will be gratuitous or possessive. A dialogue of communion can only progress in a context of freedom. With God it is the same thing. God speaks our name and, especially in our first encounters with him, waits for our free response with an infinite delicacy that seeks to dispel all our fears. This is a far cry from the *mysterium tremendum* of the sacred that human fears have projected. The wonder of the promise is that it allows us to become accustomed to the divine light of gratuitousness, gradually. "Do not fear" is the first word of every encounter between God and men from Abraham to the Virgin Mary (Gn 15:1; Is 63:1; 61:10; Lk 1:12; 1:30), and when the light of God-Love shines upon us in the face of the risen Christ, his peace is effectively given to us. "Peace be with you" (Jn 20:20).

And so, when he gives his word, God gives himself. His promise is the *gift of a presence*, the beginning of a covenant: "Bear yourself blameless in my presence, and I will make a Covenant between myself and you" (Gn 17:1-2), "I will adopt you as my own people, and I will be your God. Then you shall know that it is I, Yahweh your God" (Ex 6:7). Even in exile the Prophets reiterated this promise "Do not be afraid for I am with you" (Is 43:5). Jesus, the word who has been given to us so personally and totally that he has become ourselves, echoes this promise when he calls to his disciples in the midst of the storm: "It is I. Do not be afraid" (Jn 6:20). And again, on the point of leaving this earth for the true land of the promise, he affirms: "And know that I am with you always; yes, to the end of time" (Mt 28:20). Jesus can say this because he ushers us into the true kingdom of the Spirit where the dialogue began and where it must be completed: "And you too have been stamped with the seal of the Holy Spirit of the Promise, the pledge of our inheritance" (Eph 1:13-14).

As soon as we agree to enter into dialogue with God, we see that it is both a gift and an invitation. God does not make any speeches. He is not with us, first and foremost, as a master to teach us from the outside, as so many think to whom the very word "revelation" is repugnant. He invites us to travel with him, and he takes the path we take. He is a master of life, which is far more elating. Many people think that the active methods in teaching are a modern discovery. This is true as far as we are concerned, but God is past-master in this method, and he uses it on the level of our personal mystery: his promise sets us on the path of a *new departure*: "Leave your country, your family and your father's house, for the land I will show you" (Gn 12:1). "I came from the Father and have come into the world" (Jn 16:28). When God speaks to us it is always in view of a fresh departure, and that is why we very often prefer not to hear his voice. And yet it is only if we accept each invitation to break away that gratuitousness is revealed to us and that we reveal ourselves. A community of men that is too well established in comfort can only begin to be saved the day they show some concern for other people in other places. If man is, fundamentally, vocation, a call to go farther, it is evident that he can be saved only if he accepts to go farther. On the most spiritual level—the level on which we find inner unity—God himself is our new departure, our adventure, the new land we must set out to explore. We have no need to fear that we shall get bogged down in bourgeois comforts.

This brings us to a new realization of the infinite horizons of the promise. A promise is an assurance of something to come, and it would be childish to imagine that God is going to give us "something." What a disappointment would be in store for us. God adapted his language for the childlike mentality of the people of the Old Testament and used their images to express himself. He promised Abraham descendants and a land. But we know what bitter disappointments followed: the posterity of the house of David was never really a success and their hold on the land of the promise was always precarious, especially after the Babylonian Captivity. How are we to understand this, then? It is simply that man is always waiting for the gifts of the promise in order to take possession of them. Even on the day of the ascension the apostles still thought in those terms: "Lord, has the time come? Are you going to restore the kingdom to Israel?" (Acts 1:6). But God's plan is not to give something, but someone: himself.

God spoke in truth when he promised to make Abraham the father of a great nation and to give him the land he was living in as his own, in perpetuity (Gn 12:2; 17:8). He certainly promised him a posterity and a land, and God does not repent of his gifts (Rom 11:29) nor does he deceive us. But we can deceive ourselves. The posterity promised to Abraham is Christ (Gal 3:16) in whom all men, without distinction of racial or national origin, become sons of God: "but all of you are one in Christ Jesus" (Gal 3:29); and the land of the promise is God himself, the only heritage worthy of our spiritual condition: "Yahweh, my heritage" (Ps 16:5).

And so the promise is, forever, an invitation to man to open himself to the reality of the world of persons, to recognize the pinnacle of his own being, where he enters into communion with other personal beings, where he is no longer a thing. To accept the promise implies setting out for somewhere else, toward *someone*. Not that we have to put aside the world of things, but we have to move toward their purpose, which is to be found only in the world of persons. When we ask the Father to "give us this day our daily bread," we are expressing our hunger not only for the bread that feeds our superficial—biological, social and cultural—being but also for the Word of Life to nourish our deeper being. "Man does not live on bread alone but on every word that comes from the mouth of God" (Dt 8:3; Mt 4:4) and Jesus says: "I am the bread of life" (Jn 6:35). In the last analysis man can only be nourished by a personal presence, and the promise is the first step by which this presence is offered. If all our potential of human energy is polarized by this one passion, this one thing that is needed (Lk 10:41), all the rest, far from being pushed aside, will also find fulfillment in this: "Set your hearts on his kingdom first, and on his righteousness, and all these other things will be given you as well" (Mt 6:33).

A god who gave us everything just as we wanted it would be degrading us; it would be the false god of a primitive religious mentality. All things are offered to us for our use in the gratuitousness of creation, but it is up to us to transform them and give them to ourselves. What God is offering us in the promise is nothing less than himself, gratuitousness in person. And we can only develop a taste for this fruit of love if we leave our childish passiveness and move on to giving ourselves, thereby becoming the free creators of our own history. It seems that man's ignorance and abandonment of God have their root cause here: men expect God to be a guarantee, a protection against the difficulties of human life, and they are disappointed when he seems to contribute nothing at all. The Marxist ironically remarks that God is not necessary and "serves no purpose" in the dialectic of matter. The "believer"—who does not really believe—complains that if God really existed there would be no more suffering, as though God should be a utilitarian safety device or a kind of life insurance with infinite capital resources. The "novice" in the spiritual life, still so busy looking for God's gifts that he cannot look for God, himself, bemoans the fact that God is hidden from him. And yet, if we think about it, we realize that we would not even behave like this toward another human being for fear of reducing him to the level of a thing, a mere means to our own satisfaction. Beyond the first free gifts that God brings to us by entrusting the whole of creation to our care, he has nothing to offer: he offers only himself.

In the ongoing process of our Christian experience, therefore, the stage of the promise reveals the personal countenance of God which was still veiled in the first stage of creation. The promise is like the leading edge of history which cuts through appearances and reaches the reality of the person and of love. We can now see why, when God entrusts himself to Abraham, he also entrusts him with the whole plan of history: "Shall I conceal from Abraham what I am going to do, seeing that Abraham will become a great nation with all the nations of the earth blessing themselves by him?" (Gn 18:17). When God calls someone, it is always for the purpose of *sending* him out, not as a passive executor, but as a free man. Some attempt to avoid this, like Moses: "If it please you, my Lord, send anyone you will" (Ex 4:13), or Jeremiah: "Ah,

Lord Yahweh; look, I do not know how to speak: I am a child!"
(Jer 1:6), whereas others respond spontaneously, like Isaiah:
"Here I am, send me" (Is 6:8), or the Virgin Mary: "I am the
handmaid of the Lord, let what you have said be done to me"
(Lk 1:38). But all, without exception, feel the terrible weight
of their redemptive mission. Elijah "went on into the wilderness, a day's journey, and sitting under a furze bush wished
he were dead. 'Yahweh,' he said 'I have had enough. Take my
life; I am no better than my ancestors" (1 Kgs 19:4). This
drama will also be lived out by Jesus, God's envoy *par excel-
lence*, the given word, for the benefit of all who have been
envoys of the promise: "If a man serves me, he must follow
me...Now my soul is troubled. What shall I say: Father, save
me from this hour? But it was for this very reason that I have
come to this hour. Father, glorify your *name*!" (Jn 12:26-28).

In the context of the promise, the mission is an
annunciation. God's plan in history is not only made known
to the envoys of the word, it is entrusted to their care. And
since the seed of the promise can only bring forth its fruit of
resurrection through the cross, its heralds must also be its
protagonists. The mystery of the Church, heralding and
accomplishing God's plan in history, begins with the first
promise made to Abraham, is brought to fulfillment in Christ,
crucified and risen from the dead and is lived out by each one
of us from the moment that the word enters into our hearts
and evokes our personal response.

Faith: A Response and a Birth

If such is the word communicated to us in the promise, then
the response we give to the word is faith. The wavelength of

belief is the only one on which we, as personal mysteries, can communicate with each other. It is to be expected that faith should disappear as soon as men begin to know each other only on the lowest level as nothing more than socio-biological products. But the advent of faith is to be expected once men begin to know each other in their specifically human reality as spiritual beings with a capacity for communion with others through love.

A technician once declared that he had eliminated God from his life as he had never been able to fit him into an equation. And yet this man loved his wife and children. One might wonder if he had ever managed to get them into an equation! A personal being lies beyond the scope of measurements. We are far more than problems that can be grasped from without; we are mysteries, born from within. Before we try to listen to what the Bible tells us of the wonders of faith, we must realize that we need a certain quality of soul to open us to faith. This quality could be described as a sense of others. We can only get in touch with other people's interior reality if we welcome them into ourselves. In the last analysis we can only understand others if we love them. We can know things, even if we set aside every personal consideration, but to know persons we have to become involved and enter into communion with them. To believe is to begin to be in communion with someone. To know someone we have to believe in him and, once belief is no longer there, we can only know him from the outside.

The relation between faith and knowledge which prevails in the order of free interpersonal communion is sufficient to make us suspect that faith in God is not such a strange and inexplicable fact. Once one refuses to see God as a human projection, a product of the personal or collective conscious—in other words, an alienation—one loses one's grip on the world of things and begins to hang loose in the world of free communion in which God gives himself to us personally. How many human beings do we rub shoulders with every day who are nothing to us and to whom we are nothing? The tiny spark that would change all this would be for us to enter into relationship with them, to speak to them. But to begin a dialogue with another human being is always an adventure. We don't walk into someone's life the way we walk into a store, for in a person's life everything is free and dependant on a minimum of initial trust. This is faith.

If it is a mystery of faith to enter into a relationship with—to be born to—another human being, how much more so where God is concerned. In fact the mystery involved here is on an entirely new level since God is pure person, pure interiority. He can be known only when he approaches us freely, on his own initiative—this is the promise, in all its splendor, as we glimpsed it with regard to Abraham and Christ. Furthermore, God can be known by us only if we bid him welcome, if we tune it to the same, interior wave-length. And this is faith. Many human friendships are broken when one friend is loved by the other only for his attributes: beauty, intelligence, the security he gives, and so on. If this attribute changes, disillusionment sets in. One often hears people who have separated saying: I was mistaken in him. But it would often be nearer the truth if they acknowledged that they never really knew the other person, except from an exterior point of view, that they never really believed in him simply because he was who he was. Where God is concerned, it is even more necessary that we focus our loving faith on him simply because he is who he is . . . and not for a thousand utilitarian motives. This absolutism, which is specifically theological, can help us to appreciate that faith is not a full, speculative assent given to a certain number of truths although, often, this is all that is left of the Christian education of our childhood. Faith is an adventure in which all our powers of communion are intensely involved. Let us try and get to the heart of this drama. Because he is not a shifting, unstable person like us, God dwells in "inaccessible light" (1 Tm 6:16), beyond our reach as an object or a problem. "With him there is no such thing as alteration, no shadow of a change" (Jas 1:17), in him there is no exterior appearance. He is all inner fullness. When we communicate with others, even though we may believe in and communicate with their inner being, we do so through their exterior being. How can we enter into communion with God?

This question leads to a recognition of the full force of realism of our birth to God: faith in the living God is only possible through faith in Christ, the incarnate word of God. Islam is the most striking example of religious feeling that has brought man to the fringe of faith. But it is significant that the Muslim faith comes resolutely to a halt on the threshold of the mystery of God and refuses to go any further. For Islam it is possible to believe in God but not to enter into communion with him. On the other hand, it is only if God himself, in the fullness of his personal mystery, approaches man spontaneously and accompanies him along his way to the point of assuming all that is human in the incarnation that he can be known from man's standpoint, through the exterior signs of his humanity. Only thus is a communion between his personal mystery and ours possible. This is what comes about in Jesus Christ.

We cannot understand God's irruption into Abraham's life if we do not see in it the coming of the word into humanity. "Abraham rejoiced to think that he would see my Day; he saw it and was glad" (Jn 8:56). God's call and Abraham's answering faith are the prelude to the coming of the Son of God in the flesh. The original call and the response of faith mark the point at which God begins to be born to man and man to God. It is the burgeoning promise, the faith of betrothal that will be fulfilled in the new and eternal covenant between the incarnate word and humanity. If to love is, in a sense, to become the beloved, and if to believe is to begin to love, faith must be the drama in which God and man are born to the knowledge and love of each other. "No one has ever seen God; it is the only Son, who is nearest to the Father's heart, who has made him known" (Jn 1:18). The central fact of the promise is that God's pure interiority becomes interior to the human condition. The mysterious process that began with Abraham and his descendants is seen, in Christ, to be the path that leads to God: "I am the Way . . . if you know me, you know my Father too.... To have seen me is to have seen the Father" (Jn 14:6-8). From the moment when he first began to believe, Abraham set out to walk in the presence of the living God. "God's grace has been revealed, and it has made salvation possible for the whole human race" (Ti 2:11), and it reaches its fulfillment in Christ. The "Day" that Abraham saw in the light of his new faith was the day on which "the kindness and love of God our savior for mankind was revealed" (Ti 3:4), the day of Christ, of whose light we shall never be deprived. The promise by which God gives himself and the faith by which man receives him are both centered on the Christ-event. "God's love for us was *revealed* when God sent into the world his only Son so that we could have life through him…We ourselves have *known* and put our *faith* in God's love toward ourselves" (1 Jn 4:9, 16).

Since faith is the drama of love centered upon the person of the Lord, we can understand many aspects of its dynamic at work in us in response to the dynamic of the promise. God gives himself to Abraham and other chosen persons of the Old Testament by giving them his word. This mystery of dialogue belongs to us in Jesus Christ. We mentioned that faith demands a certain quality of soul: here, the first quality required is the capacity to listen. This is fairly rare amongst human beings. Most of what we call dialogue is, rather, two monologues in which a person expresses only himself. But we do recognize the special quality of love and friendship in which both partners know how to listen. Nothing is more liberating, and modern psychotherapy has rediscovered this deep law of communion. In the drama of our everyday lives, love cannot survive without silence. In fact the quality of the love between two people can almost be judged by the quality of their shared silence. It is not egoistical refusal to speak but a cordial openness to the other hindered by no walls of speech. In chapter twelve of Genesis we see that Abraham's first response is one of silence: he sets out without discussion. Later on, when Yahweh tells him his posterity will be as numerous as the stars of the night sky,

Abraham believes. The Virgin Mary responds with a silence of even greater depth. Once she had declared her "fiat" to God's word, she quite simply remained present to events and "pondered them in her heart" (Lk 2:19). And so, for us too, to believe in Christ is to welcome him. To "believe in his name" and "to accept him" is one and the same thing (Jn 1:12).

We must revert unceasingly to the truth that lies at the heart of our dialogue with God. Many, even deeply spiritual, people think that prayer means talking to God and, of course, it is true that even the most intimate relationship requires that we express ourselves. But it is far more important, first, to listen in prayer. Before we can reply with love we must be loved, and the first gesture of our faith is to give a welcome to him who loves us. There is nothing esoteric about this. It is simply a question of our being wholly present to the presence he offers us. Our contact with him is so uncomplicated that the use of words can only put it in danger of degenerating into a monologue on our part, and this is the most subtle form of idolatry. Pure faith is silent because it is what permits God's word to be imprinted in us. It opens us to the action of the Father, whereas all our pious prattle can only keep our attention on ourselves and distract us from him. However, it is both legitimate and necessary to express ourselves. Our words, if they are to express what is consistent and true, must be pronounced in the soberness of faith. They must be the genuine expression of a movement of the heart which involves not only feelings but our life and actions. They must be fed by the word of God who, in Christ, is expressed also in human words. In this way the Holy Spirit continues, as it were, to write the Bible in our hearts, expressing our prayers to the Father (2 Cor 3:3; Rom 8:26-27), and we really listen to God's word in our hearts when we participate in a liturgical action in which his word is proclaimed and becomes event. One can truly say that the most lyrical expression of our response to God's word is in tune with the most sober silence of faith.

If we consent to this silence of faith, then our experience truly becomes an experience of a *birth*. The promise means that we are called by our *name*. But we shall only know the full truth of our name, the truth of our unrevealed self, when we reach the end of the path that our response has set us on: "To those who prove victorious I will give the hidden manna and a white stone—a stone with a new name written on it, known only to the man that receives it.... I will inscribe on them the name of my God...and my own new name" (Rv 2:17; 3:12). When Abraham accepts the promise, he receives a new name; when Jesus becomes the acceptance of all God's promises, he receives his eternal name (Lk 1:31-32; Phil 2:9). And we, when we accept the word and "believe in his name," become "children of God" (Jn 1:12). Man receives his true name by a rebirth that molds him in the image of the son (Rom 8:29). Our baptismal name is the sacramental sign of this, but it is our whole life that has to express the eternal reality. So our name is one with our vocation, and we find the first manifestations of it in faith, for in faith we are known and loved, and in faith we live a full experience of creation (Is 43:1).

The promise *confers a presence* on us. This is so deeply true that our response to the promise cannot be an expression only of ourselves. God is present to us in such a way that our response to his gift of presence actually expresses him and ourselves in a communion. In our human loves we can see that we are still isolated as long as our response to love is only "it is I." Communion begins when one becomes capable of saying "it is thou." The prophet Hosea uses this image to tell of the restoration of the first fervent love between God and his people: "When that day comes [the day on which the first fervor of love is restored, the day of Christ]...I will say, 'You are my people' and he will answer, 'You are my God'" (Hos 2:23-25). And so, just as God "speaks" himself, in all his fullness, in the living word who fulfills his promise and in the same word "speaks" us, similarly we, who seek only him, find ourselves in our own response of faith. "Anyone who finds his life will lose it; anyone who loses his life for my sake will find it" (Mt 10:39).

This is the real uprooting that was first begun when Abraham *set out*, and it is in this context that faith is seen as the awakening of freedom. When Christ first comes into our lives and, from then on, every time we consent to hear him, we are placed under the obligation of making, for ourselves, the choice contained within the first act of creation: the choice between turning in upon ourselves or going out to others. Faith uncovers the idolatry that insinuates itself, like the serpent, into even the highest levels of our personality: "You cannot be the slave both of God and of money" (Mt 6:24). We are not free to *be* as long as we are bent on *having*. Money is only the symbol of our avarice and of our way of choosing the illusion of appearances rather than the reality of being. Faith, therefore, is the basic test of our being. It forces us to choose between being a thing and being a spiritual person. When

Abraham sets out, he turns Adam's defeat into victory. Mary's faith overcomes the original seduction to which Eve fell victim. The temptations of Christ contain all our temptations and resolve them in the freedom of grace: "Be brave: I have conquered the world" (Jn 16:33). "This is the victory over the world: our faith" (1 Jn 5:4).

In the last analysis the only victory in our lives is when we love another, and faith is the first step in this, leading us out from ourselves toward another. The real freedom toward which we are striving is the freedom of love in which the chaos of our personal endowments achieve unity and coherence is self-offering. But we can be sure of one thing: it is quite impossible for us to uproot ourselves from the ground of self unless we believe. Faith awakens the freedom within us because God does not command but invites us. He does not simply thrust on us a higher determinism but attracts us to himself in a dialogical relationship. He offers us the possibility of becoming ourselves by becoming him. This is the supreme gratuitousness of love. The Bible expresses this awakening to the light of love by a word which has, unfortunately, taken on a very different meaning for most people today: Justice. Genesis says "Abram put his faith in Yahweh, who counted this as making him justified" (Gn 15:6). This is the beginning of the new creation for, if believing means to begin to exist for the one who offers his love, then faith is the beginning of a love that is destined to transform life. Faith is a "conversion" of one's whole being toward him who loves, a turning-back of the heart to him. "The kingdom of God is close at hand. Repent, and believe the Good News" (Mk 1:15). In human love we can see this: the advent of the one we

love causes us to "turn" toward him and away from our solitude. He who loves awakes to a second creation in which his
original being finds a new unity. The conversion operated by
love polarizes all the inherent qualities of a person, and the
more he loves the more he fulfills himself in his turning
toward another. The discovery, through love, of God can
bring about a new birth far more profound and all-encom-
passing than any discovery through love of another human
being. The whole of our human potentiality, focused on him,
is renewed and unified. This is the "justification" that he operates in us by adjusting and ordering the whole of our being in
a unity that is far more than a fragile, moral equilibrium
because it is unity in love, which is himself.

"The upright man will live by his faithfulness" (Hb
2:4; Gal 3:11). The justice of the Gospels is the "uprightness"
of love that no external legislation, however spiritual, can
ever bring about (Gal 3:11-12). Only he who is love can spark
our free response to his promise. Faith is this free response
in which our deepest self wells up and says "yes" to God's
offer of himself. Not that faith "justifies" us by permitting us
to find our own balance within ourselves, but it becomes the
way God takes to become our way and the bond of integrity
that unifies the love within us. As we saw earlier, when God
offers his word and we accept his offer, we are born to him
and he is born in us, in love. Our experience of Christ is,
through our faith in him, the experience of a birth to freedom
and love and leads us into the harmony of the Godhead. But
we must not forget that this harmony is not an object that
we can own. The law of grace is diametrically opposed to
the law of quantities. God's plan for the world is a plan of

personalization, and we are going to have to believe for as long as we live. It is never done, once for all. Love cannot stop short without denying itself: love is a birth, and the faith that engenders love is a constant and ever-new choice to fulfill ourselves in another rather than settling back into ourselves.

"The upright man will live by his faithfulness," not by high ideals or moral imperatives. He lives by Someone. Faith can be the leaven of our lives, if we are willing constantly to correct the waywardness of our congenital hunger by directing it toward Christ (Jn 6:35). In him we shall find all the beauty of all love, both human and divine. Perhaps we have sometimes been struck by a certain quality of youthfulness that seems to be always new in the life of a couple or of two friends whose vision of each other has been purified by time in the light of a love that unites them. Since the gift that lies dormant in the promise is the one presence that is capable of satisfying our love, it can never be simply an object. So our faith must be a kind of continual movement from the gifts to the Giver. And this is true of all love, whether human or divine. Ultimately, there is only one love in which the whole of the Christian experience is lived. The wonder wrought by Christ is that he raises the whole of our experience to the level of faith, and hence no beauty can satisfy us unless we strive with all our being toward the personal countenance from which all beauty flows.

HOPE CREATES HISTORY

And so our life story and that of all humanity is lived out in a state of tension. To say that the "upright man will live by his faithfulness" is to say that the strength of love lies in a presence. But how can this be so when we are constantly confronted with such emptiness, such an impression of "absence" in our own personal and social chaos? There is a tremendous distance to be traveled between the first awakening of faith and the point at which we reach the full freedom of love. Many give up on the way, forgetting that the sun will rise only at the end of a long night or, knowing this, fearful of the dark road that precedes the dawn. They conclude that freedom does not really exist and that there is no such thing as a happy love. What do they need? Faith? Perhaps they have had faith and it has been stifled by disappointment? What they seem to need is the realism that goes with faith and that makes us able to believe not just once but every day anew, weaving our belief into the passage of time so that we grow stronger with the strength of a living man. They lack the impetus of faith which, instead of losing momentum in the course of events, faces up to events and gathers them up in its own movement toward freedom. This power of faith which creates history is hope.

Abraham's nascent faith would have remained barren if it had not been tempered by the shocks of life. At the beginning, the experience of creation took the form of a poem, a love story and a drama. The promise enters men's hearts like the first song sung by the word of God, and it is echoed by men's first personal response. But before the promise can bear the fruit of communion in men, they need to be put to the test. Our capacity for disinterested love has to prove itself. "This love of yours is like a morning cloud, like the dew that quickly disappears…. What I want is love, not sacrifice; knowledge of God, not holocausts" (Hos 6:4-6). In

95

hope, faith becomes fidelity that lasts in *time*. In hope, love becomes a presence through *signs*. Time, which can wear down as well as create, and signs, which can hide as well as reveal, are the two elements in our personal history that will prove conclusive in the forging of hope.

We have seen that to live according to promise is to live with a seed that has been planted in our hearts. Time is God's patience that has confidence in man and collaborates in his maturing. It is not a question of chance that there is a delay in the fulfillment of the promise, for it follows the pace of our growth. As an illustration of this we should read the accounts of the first trials endured by Abraham and by the envoys of the Old Testament in the light of the Gospel passages in which Jesus declares himself to be the true seed of life in mankind (Gn 15:1-12; 22; Ex 32; 2 Sm 7; 1 Kgs 19; Jn 20:7-18; Is 63:7–64:11 and Mt 13; Jn 12:23-28; 1 Cor 3:5-9). This theme of the mystery of time seen as the unfolding of hope underlies the whole saga of our pasch, and we shall come across it again and again. But here we can look at it, within the context of the slow accomplishment of the promise, as the test of weariness that calls for a constant, creative fidelity.

It is relatively easy for someone who loves to promise or "give his word." It is far more difficult to prove that one really does love by keeping one's word, in other words, by giving oneself. But is it not unrealistic to promise fidelity, especially to God? Who can guarantee that he will keep his promise? Certainly it would be presumptuous to think that we can ever guarantee this for ourselves, but as soon as we begin to count on God to ensure our fidelity, we are awakening to hope. Hope means to count on him and on his love no matter what happens. "We may be unfaithful but He is always faithful. . . . I know who it is that I have put my trust in, and I have no doubt at all that he is able to take care of all that I have entrusted to him" (2 Tm 2:13; 1:12). Just as faith can be seen in the free gift of God and our own free response, so hope can be seen in our confidence both in him and in our own effective contribution. When we love God, just as when we love others, we become a promise that we cannot fulfill alone: we need him to come and fulfill it in us and with us.

And so hope is revealed, by the test of time, to be the power of gratuitousness concealed in a nascent faith. Instead of consuming faith like a fleeting infatuation, time, fecundated by hope, entrenches it firmly in our lives because Christ, the fullness of time and the fountainhead of everlasting life, is ours (Jn 4:14). Time, as we experience it in our daily lives, is an invitation to eternity. It is the new rhythm of the promise, inviting us to discard the surface of our own activity and go deeper, to the level of the Spirit who lies at the heart of our lives (Gal 5:25).

> We can boast about our sufferings. These sufferings bring patience, as we know, and patience brings perseverance, and perseverance brings hope, and this hope is not deceptive, because the love of God has been poured into our hearts by the Holy Spirit which has been given us. (Rom 5:3-5)

The same movement, from the surface to the underlying current of personal life, takes place in hope through signs. True love can survive only in a climate of transparent interiority, but this finds expression in signs. This is the whole meaning of our exteriority in relation to each other, and it is the significance of Christ, the incarnate word, in our relation to God. But signs can both reveal and conceal. If we stop short at the sign and fail to recognize the person that it expresses, we thrust the person back into his solitude. If on the other hand we reach what is beyond the sign, we find ourselves face to face with another person and able to communicate in a new joy and a new life. Jesus experienced the ambivalence of signs, tragically, in his own life. He was the living, human sign of God's love: "But, as I have told you, you can see me and still you do not believe" (Jn 6: 36). To see in order to believe; to believe in order to be born to the knowledge of another: this is the whole import of signs, and it contains, in embryo, the drama of our paschal liberation.

The word "sign," preferred by John (Jn 2:11; 6:14; 7:31; 12:37; 20:30), and the word "miracle," preferred by the other evangelists, both refer to the same biblical reality. A certain kind of apologetics, unduly influenced by rationalism, sees a miracle as an extraordinary sign contrary to the laws of nature and made in order to prove something. The biblical point of view is rather different. Extraordinary or not, the miracle is destined to "astonish" the beholder and to open a way to his heart. The first discovery of a scientific phenomenon is always astonishing, but how much more full of wonder is the first discovery of another living person. It is true that we can only know others by loving them, but we still need a certain capacity for astonishment and wonder. Wonder is very much akin to faith, and how can we believe if we are blasé? The signs of communion between human beings are destined, constantly, to renew our capacity for wonder: they feed love by rejuvenating the eyes of faith. Christ is the sign of wonder who speaks of the communion between God and men. Every miracle is a glimpse of the light of his personal mystery and not just a proof for the use of apologists. Biblical signs—and Christ is the supreme sign who sums up all the others—are events that shake men from their complacent torpor, calling to them and inviting them to wonder. "Truly, Yahweh is in this place and I never knew it!" (Gn 28:16). The miracle given us in Christ is meant to open our hearts to a presence.

In this regard perhaps more than in any other, we must read the gospel with the intelligence, not of the flesh, but of the Spirit. All the signs of the Old Testament, from those of the Patriarchs to the Exodus and the Prophets, are fulfilled in the signs worked by Christ and, above all, in himself. But the miracles of the Gospels are not related simply in order that we may believe in what is past. They also teach us something, in the present, about the durable meaning of the exterior world in which we live. Jesus' miracles are, today, because they reveal through exterior signs that have changed the action of the unchanging Spirit. From the very first stirring of creation this action has always been to render all exterior reality transparent to the interior reality of love. This applies equally to the material world working out its destiny and waiting for our liberation, to our bodies caught up in the hope of redemption, to our relations with others always in need of a new and deeper intimacy; and finally this applies to our personal, interior unification which gradually progresses toward a perfect harmony between what we are and what we appear to be. If it is true that the promise actualizes, on the most personal level, all the latent potentialities of creation, then it is true to say that its dynamic is the dynamic of hope. It is in hope that the outward signs of creation make the transition to interiority and reach their ultimate meaning in the world of love and of the person.

The hope of the Gospels is more than the conjectures or wishes formulated by someone in distress. It is not a purely psychological phenomenon, even though an analogy can be drawn between creative fidelity and hope. The dimensions of hope are as great as the dimensions of the world and of history, of man and of God. Hope is the highest point man can reach in giving a welcome to God. It is a participation in the all-powerful love that can accomplish far more "than we can ask or imagine" (Eph 3:20). Hope is the fullness of being in which our personal mystery finds its new center in the Other. In hope, the radical poverty of our being becomes our capacity to be filled to the brim with the gifts of love. Suicide is the clearest possible expression of the absence of hope, for by it a man tired of the struggle to possess a communion that forever eludes him finds himself clinging only to the emptiness of self and gives up in the face of this absurdity. Hope is the key to the meaning of all personal, community and cosmic history because it is man's supreme gratuitousness reconciled with God's. But it will not teach the meaning of history to idle spectators. It is by our involvement in hope that we create our own history and the history of the world. From Abraham, who hoped against hope and thus became "the father of many nations" (Rom 4:18) to ourselves who "believe in him who raised Jesus our Lord from the dead" (Rom 4:24), man's salvation has been an object of hope (Rom 8:24). But we must understand that the object of hope does not lie in an absolute future, as in Jewish Messianism. It has already begun to be fulfilled since the risen Christ, the first fruits of the new creation that Abraham looked forward to, has passed through death to life. Our Christian experience occurs in the context of a promise which has already seen effective fulfillment in Christ. It is our faith in him which awakens us to freedom, but it is our hope in him that will draw us on to the fullness of freedom. "May the God of our Lord Jesus Christ, the Father of glory, give you a spirit of wisdom and perception of what is revealed, to bring you to full knowledge of him. May he enlighten the eyes of your mind so that you can see what hope his call holds for you..." (Eph 1:17-18).

CHAPTER FOUR

The Pasch, the Springtime of Love

Our Christian experience is an experience of integral liberation which draws everything, from the cosmos to the spirit, toward God the fullness of love. Listening to what the Bible has to say about the fact of creation that gives us all the basic ingredients of our existence, we discovered signs of the initial gratuitousness that calls them into being. In a second step we saw, in the promise, that same gratuitousness offering itself to us and awakening our freedom not as in a teaching process but as the very presence of God who solicits a welcome. His offer and our response engage us in a common destiny, and a tremendous hope is opened to us. This hope is already a liberation. But what does this liberation consist of?

Anyone who has a responsibility for teaching others, particularly children, should ask himself this question: what is liberation? If we want to guide someone to maturity, we have to help him to free himself progressively and to acquire the habit of living on the level of the spirit in a harmonious relationship with others. To begin with, we have to be realistic and accept an unformed personality for what it is. It is essential that we recognize the gratuitousness hidden in the basic elements of a personality if we ever hope to foster its full and harmonious development. This is the first step—the step of creation. But then there is an awakening of the young person's freedom in a dialogue, and this will develop only if there is a climate of acceptance, trust and understanding and if there is a reciprocal commitment to the same task. This is the step of the promise. It is here that the real process of liberation actually begins.

In God's method of teaching us, it is this point of liberation that we begin to reach the goal we are always in search of, even when it goes unsaid: inner balance and unity. We are forever groping for a balanced synthesis of the component parts of our lives. We seek to fulfill ourselves, knowing that it is not easy to be oneself, that it has to be the fruit of a becoming. And to become oneself, in the full flowing of all one's potentialities, means to establish a deep-seated harmony between oneself and others. We all experience brief periods of integration and inner balance, and these give us some idea of the end toward which we are moving. But between the possibilities inherent in the beginnings and the peak of fulfillment the road is long and hard. This is the road of our liberation, the passage from the first awakening of freedom in dialogue and faith to the full freedom of the adult.

What exactly does it mean to be free? Idealist philosophies—which have sometimes affected existentialism also—cannot really help us here. From experience we can say that freedom is the state in which we are most fully ourselves with no coercion whatever from without. In other words, it is the state in which we live gratuitously. To be free means to be fully oneself, to be gratuitous, to love and be in common with others and at peace with oneself. This experience of freedom means, first of all, that the seeds of freedom lie within us but are not yet developed. Freedom is essentially the *fruit of a process of liberation*. It is not simply the abstract possibility to choose. And so our liberation works itself out in a gradual overcoming of whatever hinders the spontaneous flowering of our gratuitousness. It is never completed, it can always grow, since gratuitousness is infinite and eternally youthful like the love it pours forth.

To become free, then, is to fulfill the promise implicit in the awakening of our liberty. In fact, if we read what the Bible tells us of the promise in the time of the Patriarchs and later, we see that the community of destiny that unites God and man in a reciprocal bond of giving in the word and in faith leads to a twofold objective: a land and a posterity. A land of freedom and posterity of free men: "Know this for certain, that your descendants will be exiles in a land not their own, where they will be slaves…. In the fourth generation they will come back here…. To your descendants I will give this land" (Gn 16:13-18). When one sees how this twofold theme is developed throughout the Bible, one cannot help but see that this text is the promise of a blessed posterity which counts all humanity set free in the risen Christ (Gal 3:25-5:6) and of a new earth in which life will flow as a free gift (Rv 21:1-7). The time of liberation runs from the first promises to their final accomplishment. The Bible describes it as a "covenant" which works itself out progressively in history, image of our personal, community and universal liberation which is reached, progressively, by our learning to live in peace with ourselves, with other people and with all of reality. Thus all harmony flows, as a free gift, from man's oneness with freedom in person, God.

Exodus sketches the first rough outline of the promised liberation. The work of Moses is the beginning of fulfillment of the patriarchal promises concerning the land and the nation. The nation lies in bondage, the land has still to be conquered. Moses' work is, first and foremost, one of liberation and of conquest, and this is expressed in the word "pasch," understood in the Christian tradition as meaning a "passage." Passage, first, of the Red Sea (Ex 14) and, by extension, from Egypt to the promised land, symbolizing the passage from slavery to freedom. Christ will be the final accomplishment of the mosaic pasch by passing, personally, from the slavery of death to the freedom of life, taking with him all of Abraham's descendants—"the scattered children of God" (Jn 11:52)— from the slavery of sin and death to the true land of freedom, the land of Love (Rom 4:20-23; 1 Jn 3:14). Jesus' resurrection thus fulfills all the promises (Acts 13:32-33).

SLAVERY IN A FOREIGN LAND

The story of God's people, symbolizing our own story and that of all humanity, begins with the experience of slavery in a foreign land. It would be useless for us to want to move from childhood to maturity with no recognition of the slavery and alienation that hold us captive. Slavery was first forced upon the consciousness of the people of Israel by the brutal reality of physical violence, and they perceived it in accordance with the mentality and the social structures of their times, two thousand years before Jesus Christ (Ex 1, 2). The Israelites were a minority group with no strong tribal cohesiveness who had immigrated to the Nile delta with the support of foreign influence, and they suddenly found themselves victim of a resurgence of nationalism and of a new dynasty and reduced to the condition of slaves. A long time later, after the return from the Babylonian Captivity in about the fifth century B.C., Israel acquired a new perception of the fact of slavery on a more spiritual and also on a more universal level. And this new perception of the fundamental slavery in which mankind is held captive is portrayed in the story of man's banishment from the paradise of freedom, in chapter three of Genesis. Finally, to mention only one New Testament text, Paul expresses his synthesis of both experiences—that of the Jews under the Mosaic law and that of humanity—when he writes to the Romans of man's experience of being captive to a disposition toward sin (Rom 7:23).

Some of the more obvious findings of modern psychology can bring considerable light to bear upon the details of Paul's densely packed and dramatic affirmations. Our first servitude can be seen as, simply, the anarchy of our personal gifts and talents. If it is true to say that "everyone who commits sin is a slave" (Jn 8:34), it is also true to say that behind our personal, actual sins is a background of a capacity, a tendency to sin. And this is our first slavery, the Egypt from which we must free ourselves. Also, like the Old Testament which speaks of the Serpent and the Devil, Paul speaks of sin as though the weakness in us that offers resistance to the spirit and to love—and thus to God—could be personified

(Rom 5:12 ref. Gn 3:1; Wis 2:24). But what is the original of this divisiveness within us? "Once, when there was no Law, I was alive" (Rom 7:9): the child within us bewails that time of happy irresponsibility when we were ignorant of life. "What a wretched man I am!" (Rom 7:24). It would be so much easier to allow oneself to be lived by life and determined by one or another of one's initial tendencies without having to judge and choose in order to make them all work together toward a higher unity. It would be so much easier…yes, but it would be a refusal of the adventure of life.

We should not be surprised if we feel that it is too hard to conquer our freedom and if we experience a kind of nostalgic longing for the security of servitude just as Israel, afraid of the rigors of the desert, bemoaned the good leeks of Egypt. This tendency is a good indication of where our fundamental sin lies, and a little psychology can help us to see that it consists in living the different levels of our being anarchically and without integration into a harmonious whole. We could well examine our consciences on this level and try to uncover the roots—and not only the manifestations—of our personal sins. The raw material of our personalities made up of impulses, instincts, tendencies, which are all good in themselves and a response to life. But we cannot be reduced to an impulse or an instinct without being reduced to something less than ourselves. Another cluster of potentialities takes shape within us with the forming of a social self and here too each element, though good in itself, cannot be expected to express the whole of our personality without completely distorting it. Then comes the first reflexive movement of consciousness, a first attempt to grope for interior unity and arbitrate between the rival tendencies and life-forces within us. If we do no more than attempt to reach a balance between the two poles of our personality, we fall far below ourselves into an ethic of self-interest that leaves no room for the higher values of love and gratuitousness. It is this kind of "average humanity" that La Fontaine derides in his tales of animals that talk, for on this level man is no more than a talking animal, an embryonic consciousness groping to reconcile the demands of the individual and of the biological group. Much of human behavior, in fact, stems from this ethic. Even religious behavior is sometimes no more than the expression of a biological or sociological pressure.

Over and above these three levels of the substructure of personality lies a network of unconscious constraint: the *id* which is somewhat analogous to the "double" of animist religions. This *id* is the seat of our instinctive life and the *super-ego*, which is the custodian of social and educational imperatives and of our habits. The final arbitration will then be a step beyond the *ego*, a fully conscious choice that unifies all the different levels of life and orients them toward personal values. Only on this level can one go beyond the *ego* to the *self*, and this is the freedom that lies at the end of our journey.

Is this not the meaning of Paul's cry of anguish, "I cannot understand my own behavior. I fail to carry out the things I want to do, and I find myself doing the very things I hate…. Instead of doing the good things I want to do, I carry out the sinful things I do not want" (Rom 7:15-19)? Paul has a bitter experience of the necessary struggle to reach beyond the ego to the unity of self. When he says, "I," he speaks of the fine point of this conscious self drawn to the higher values, in this case, to what is holy: "In my inmost self I dearly love God's Law, but I can see that my body follows a different law [that is: a different behavior]" (Rom 7:22-23). That which he calls his "unspiritual self" or "the sin which lives inside my body," he usually speaks of as the "body" or as "nature." Paul, however, is not saying that the body, nature or matter are evil, as many undeclared Jansenists or Manichees still believe. He is simply using the ancient, psychological categories (body, soul and spirit), according to which the body, of "the flesh," simply means the body and soul of a man divorced from the spirit. The "natural man" is one who is weak and divided in himself, "deprived of God's glory," as compared to the "spiritual man" who lives the life of spiritual values and of God. This conflict is not a pure figure of speech or a psychological fantasy. It is part of our daily spiritual experience.

To be oneself is seen, then, as being the fine point of oneself turned toward others in a free gesture of love: this is the lifeline of our personality. To the extent to which a part of our interior potential is severed from this lifeline, it falls back into a chaotic existence and is "condemned to death" (Rom 7:24). This is our sin. The slavery in which we are held is fundamentally a division within ourselves, and it is one and the same division that separates us from God. It is because gratuitousness and love are not abstract ideas but are God that, when any of our innate potentialities deviates from this lifeline, we are knocked off balance. Gratuitousness cannot be our gyroscope if it is simply a value. It must be a presence. A person can only establish a communion with another person; anything less than this would lead him to a vacuum. The traces of original sin within us are precisely the signs of the lack of this presence in the lifeline of our personality. This is why we are separated from ourselves to the extent to which we are separated from God. Our land of freedom is love, and love is someone. If he is not with us, we are in bondage in a foreign land far from home.

The results of this basic imbalance are evident in our lives. First of all we are alienated by material creation which becomes human only to the extent to which we recapture our interior freedom (Rom 8:19-22). We are also alienated by our bodies which can only find balance in accord with the Spirit (Rom 8:23; 1 Cor 6:12-20). But we are alienated most of all by others who remain strangers and objects to be dominated until we can recognize them as subjects whom we can love and with whom we can be in communion (1 Jn 1 and 2). Taken as a whole, sin is a slavery that divides us on all levels. It is very important for our Christian experience that we throw off the mask that conceals the untruth and seduction of sin (Gn 3:13; Rom 7:11). It takes over what is good—for everything in our deepest yearnings, in our bodies and in the world is good—in order to trick us into believing that we can become "as gods" (Gn 3:5) by fulfilling one or another aspect of ourselves without love. The seduction of sin is to transform the gratuitousness latent in all things into possessiveness, whereas the kingdom of God can be possessed only by the humble of heart (Mt 5:3) who live not for self but for him and for others. Through Jesus, the supreme example of poverty, the gratuitousness of God and of others is restored to us: "And the reason he died for all was so that living men should live no longer for themselves, but for him who dies and was raised to life for them" (2 Cor 5:15).

The slavery of sin is a slavery of lies and of darkness (Jn 8:31-47) which, turning us back to possessiveness, becomes opposition, hatred and egoism. It is exactly the opposite of the light and love in which John contemplates the beauty of God (1 Jn 1:5-7; 4:7-9).

THE PASCHAL LIBERATION

Such is our original condition of slavery, and it is in direct relation to the fact that we are called to a life in the spirit and in love. It is in every respect the replica in the negative of the positive picture of our passage to freedom. The first condition we must fulfill to arrive at freedom is that we be lucidly, pitilessly and peacefully *sincere*. To be free we must first recognize that we are not free. Not everybody really accepts this. We cannot be sincere unless we really want to be, and one of the things we all find repugnant is to accept the truth about ourselves. Either we avoid looking squarely at ourselves or if circumstances and particularly other people confront us with the truth about ourselves we refuse to accept it. Sometimes this refusal is very subtly expressed: much of our sadness, bitterness and discouragement conceal a refusal to accept the reality of our situation. We are always willing to believe that we are our "ideal self," and it is painful for us to have to admit that our real self is not very "ideal." This is why we not only have to be clear sighted in truth, we also have to be peaceful, for peace is the sign that the objectiveness of our view is on the level of our hearts. Peace, after all, follows on combat—the combat against our interior state of division.

One of the first conditions of liberation is to recognize that one is a sinner—not just that one has committed a certain number of sins. Since sin is untruth and seduction, our healing begins with a sense of humor that allows us to recognize the trickery of sin and with the humility that accepts it as such.

"It is not those who are well who need the doctor, but the sick. I have not come to call the virtuous, but sinners to repentance" (Lk 5:31-32). And so, after curing the man born blind, symbol of our own journey into light, Jesus could declare, "It is for judgment that I have come into this world, so that those without sight may see"—this, we can easily understand, but then he goes on, paradoxically: "'and those with sight turn blind.' Hearing this, some Pharisees who were present said to him, 'We are not blind, surely?' Jesus replied: 'Blind? If you were, you would not be guilty, but since you say, "We see," your guilt remains'" (Jn 9:30-40). We have difficulty understanding this: our sin will always be with us if we maintain the pretense of all the religious and philosophical systems that fail to recognize the original bondage in which men's hearts are held and which, therefore, can never set us free. On the other hand, the experience of psychotherapy shows that a first step in a cure of mind is that the sick person acknowledge that he is split by internal conflict. On the level of the whole man, this is the way of the divine therapy: it offers us light, and if we allow that light to shine into us, our eyes of faith are opened in truth and humility and we begin to be free.

It is important that we understand the open and loving orientation of this truth about ourselves. It is very far from being a coldly objective diagnosis to which we must simply resign ourselves. In the very act of recognizing our sin, we enter the presence that frees us from it. Our sin is egoism because it is a lie, but the light we throw upon it restores us to love. Our sin encloses us in a cold solitude: a humble faith opens us to the warm light of his presence. Faith in Jesus-Savior is our salvation because, first and foremost, it is truth on the level of the heart which opens us to him. "You will learn the truth and the truth will make you free" (Jn 8:32-36). Humility is probably the most misunderstood of all Christian values. From Celsus to Nietzsche, and in all ideologies of power, there have always been people who have had an allergic reaction to humility. And it is obvious that many Christians who are not yet "spiritual" live in a caricature of humility. Truth is not something that can be mimed. To be free in truth is to be oneself in the spontaneity of love, and seen in this light humility is seen to be the first breakthrough of freedom. It does not abase us. Quite the contrary, only if we recognize that we still fall far short of gratuitousness can we hope to attain it. Humility exalts us (Lk 18:14) not by self-glorification but by opening us to the personal love that lies concealed within servitude. The humility of faith is the first step in our paschal liberation because it is heavy with the everlasting springtime of love.

Springtime—this too is someone: Christ, the first-fruits of all who will rise from the dead (1 Cor 15:20-23). This brings us to the second condition for becoming free: *we cannot become free alone*. Ultimately, we are always set free by someone else. This is not to say that the personal movement which leads us to maturity is not our own. Nothing could set us free in spite of ourselves, and to become oneself is precisely to fulfill one's own personality. But experience shows that this inner pasch also leans heavily on a presence which is other than ourself and which makes our pasch possible. We saw how, in the first awakening of our liberty, a presence in dialogue and faith is necessary. A presence is still necessary in the first movement of liberation in which we integrate our different potentialities in unity. The problem is how can another person, who is by definition other than ourselves, be necessary for us to become ourselves? How can another have a part in our own movement of liberation and not be a constraint?

The answer lies in the very gratuitousness which is our liberation. Another person can share in the first thrust of our own liberation to the extent to which he loves us. Everyone knows what it means to have someone who loves him come into his life. The full freedom of self-sharing, in which one reaches complete fulfillment, is not immediately established. This is done at a later stage. Before that there has to be an initial liberation by a gesture that welcomes us, a love that is freely given to us. Every day, all around us, we see proof of the fact that those who are least free are those who have been the least loved. This lesson of modern life simply reiterates God's eternal teaching: for a man to be healed and freed from the bondage of sin, it is not enough for him to have a clear vision of the evil that grips him; he must also know that he is loved. In the last analysis, nothing can change until he begins to live in a new gratuitousness in which he feels himself to be respected and loved for himself.

This is the way in which Christ is our pasch. He sets us free not from afar but from within the very source of ourselves. We begin to be free when we find that we are loved in spite of all the bonds that still prevent us from loving freely in return. No man, only God within us, can do this. As his presence does not inhibit or exclude our own, he is able to offer himself at the very roots of our spontaneous growth so that he can become the keynote of our life. The purest blending in harmony of the divine and the human is Christ. When we give him welcome in faith, we begin to be free because we are welcoming into the source of our being the personal wellspring of freedom. He is freedom itself because he is love and there can be neither intrusion nor alienation in him. Anyone who has known a true love can tell of the unexpected unity and deep peace that he suddenly experiences from the moment he is certain that he is loved and welcomed for himself. And if this new peace takes possession of the farthest depths of our inner being, in which the presence of another human being could only be experienced as a violation, then we can have some idea of the perfect harmony we are groping toward through our present chaos. To believe in Christ means to give him welcome but, even more, it means to be welcomed by him. Faith is the first covenant and the assurance of being loved from which springs our very being at every moment. "Those who are in Christ Jesus are not condemned [that is to say: enslaved in a foreign land].... For I am certain of this: neither death nor life, no angel, no prince, nothing that exists, nothing still to come, not any power, or height or depth, nor any created thing, can ever come between us and the love of God made visible in Christ Jesus our Lord" (Rom 8:1; 8:38-39). Christ is our pasch and the springtime of love, and the trust he places in us and the love he pours out on us are what we need to launch us into the full freedom of loving. The sap of love has brought forth shoots of life, and we can rest assured that they will flower and bear fruit (Gal 5:22 f).

Christ fulfills the promises of the first, Mosaic pasch when he becomes our springtime. The Book of Exodus speaks, in chapter one, of the bondage of God's people in Egypt, symbolizing our bondage in sin. It then goes on to speak of Moses, the figure of Christ. The second chapter, in a didactic tradition apparent in many Old Testament writings, is built on an interpretation of two names. Pharaoh's daughter gives the foundling child the name of Moses "because, she said, I drew him out of the water" (Ex 2:10), and later Moses gives his own son the name of Gershom because, he says, "I am a stranger in a foreign land" (Ex 2:22). The two fundamental traits of the promise are thus present in the person of the first liberator of God's people: a posterity that has been saved from slavery, and the land into which it has been led. In Christ, in whom we enter into God's land, we also became God's children in freedom. The first fifteen chapters of the Book of Exodus tell how the first pasch came about, and the main events which took place. In the first movement of love by which God frees us, he *remembers* his covenant (Ex 2:24). This is the foundation for our certitude of faith: God's faithfulness is tireless and overwhelmingly touching (1 Cor 1:1-9). God's remembrance of us is not in reference to the past, it is always a presence.

God reveals that he is *holy*: "Take off your shoes, for the place on which you stand is holy ground" (Ex 3:5). An innate fear, which often paralyzes our will to open up to God, is allayed in the wonder of being called and of being loved. Moses says, "I must go and look at this strange sight" (Ex 3:3), and his gesture is a sign of the movement that takes place in the pasch when we are drawn "out of the darkness into his wonderful light" (1 Pt 2:9). To approach the heart of the fire that burns without being consumed is to become holy with God's holiness (Lev 19:2; 2 Cor 1:12). The culminating point of the process of liberation has already been revealed as the absolutely gratuitous act of *worship*: "After you have led the people out of Egypt, you are to offer worship to God on this mountain" (Ex 3:12). This is the adoration of God, in spirit and in truth, that the Father asks of us (Jn 4:12-24), the absolute of gratuitousness, loving admiration and the praise of his glory (1 Pt 2:9).

God does not set us free from afar. He is close to us and communicates his *name* to us, symbolizing the secret of his personal, life-giving mystery (Ex 3:13-15). The covenant or contract is thus sealed in our inner being: "I have made your name known to them and will continue to make it known, so that the love with which you loved me may be in them, and so that I may be in them" (Jn 17:26).

The *plagues* that afflict Pharaoh and his people, due to the seasonal changes in Egypt (Ex 7-11), are signs of this conquering presence. Jesus brings these signs to fulfillment in his own saving signs, the miracles he works to open men's hearts to the coming of the kingdom of love. In the kingdom men will be saved by being reconciled both within themselves and with each other after divisiveness, the work of the Devil, has been cast out (Lk 11:20).

The *memorial* meal of the pasch, incorporating the ancient rites, consecrating new life (the firstborn of the flock: the paschal lamb and the firstfruits of the harvest: the unleavened bread), is the liturgical celebration of God's coming to his people in this new springtime of life (Ex 12-13). Jesus, true "lamb of God who takes away the sins of the world" (Jn 1:29) and "firstfruits" of the new life (1 Cor 15:20-23), brings us into the land of our first freedom: "He loves us and he washed away our sins with his blood, and made us a line of kings, priests to serve his God and Father" (Rv 1:5-6); "Make yourselves into a completely new batch of bread, unleavened as you are meant to be. Christ, our pasch, has been sacrificed; let us celebrate the feast, then . . . having only the unleavened bread of sincerity and truth" (1 Cor 5:7-8). The feast we celebrate is our continual rebirth to the love which is bestowed on us.

In the different stages of the passage from Egypt to the Promised Land we can read the story of our own passage into life through *baptism*. Israel's passage through the Red Sea brings them out of bondage (Ex 14): our passage through the waters of baptism brings us out of the bondage of sin. The fact that this liberation has already taken place, once for all time, does not mean that it is an event of the past. It is present to us, always, because it is someone who is present: "Death has no power over him any more. When he died, he died, once for all, to sin, so his life now is life with God: and in that way, you too must consider yourselves to be dead to sin but alive for God in Christ Jesus" (Rom 6:9-11).

God speaks to us through events. He saves us, also, not in figures of speech but in fact. The events of the Mosaic pasch were figurative (1 Cor 10:1-6), but the great event of light and love which saves us is the risen Christ. The first requirement for faith, setting out on the path of liberation, is to know "Christ and the power of his resurrection and to share his sufferings" (Phil 3:10). "The life I now live in this body I live in faith: faith in the Son of God who loved me and who sacrificed himself for my sake" (Gal 2:20). The saga of the first pasch is often recalled in the Old Testament as the supreme event by which God manifested himself "in the *power of his right hand*." And here again he does not save his people from afar, "For I, Yahweh, your God, I am holding you by the right hand; I tell you, 'Do not be afraid; I will help you.'" (Is 41:13). "For Zion was saying, 'Yahweh has abandoned me, the Lord has forgotten me.' Does a woman forget her baby at the breast, or fail to cherish the son of her womb? Yet even if these forget, I will never forget you. See, I have branded you on the palms of my hands...." (Is 49:14-16). And now our wounds are forever engraved on the hands of his son and how could we doubt of his love? "Look, here are my hands. . . . Doubt no longer but believe" (Jn 20:27). For it is ultimately in the reality of the Cross that the Lord "bares his holy arm in the sight of all the nations" (Is 52:10). It is always an extraordinary experience to be loved: "Who could believe what we have heard, and to whom has the power of Yahweh been revealed?" (Is 53:1). God's power of love is revealed in Christ on the Cross (1 Cor 1:24). "Is my hand too short to redeem?" (Is 50:2). In Christ's pasch God reaches out his hand to us and, like Jairus' daughter, we rise up and come back to life (Mt 9:25).

And so the first step in our passage to freedom is taken in the humility of faith, opening us to the inexhaustible fountain of life in the love that is offered us. This is our invincible hope. In this hope the spinning out of time will reveal the fecundity of our faith. "And this hope is not deceptive, because the love of God has been poured into our hearts by the Holy Spirit which has been given us" (Rom 5:5). The very first liberation offered us is not of a legal nature, like a debt that is cancelled, nor of a moral nature, like the trust we put in someone's promise. It is ontological, mystical and existential: it is an authentic infusion of new life—a new life that is someone. Christ, our pasch, is portrayed in the Old Testament as shepherd of his people, but he is a unique shepherd, for "I have come so that they may have life and have it to the full. I am the good shepherd: the good shepherd is one who lays down his life for his sheep" (Jn 10:10-11). Once again: he does not give life from afar, he gives us his own life: "From his fullness we have, all of us, received—yes, grace in return for grace" (Jn 1:16).

Consequently, the wonderful thing about this Christian experience is that, at its roots, it consists in becoming ourselves while, at the same time, becoming him. This is the eternal aspiration of all true love. It is specifically, the action of the risen Christ, through the constant "nowness" of our baptism, that brings us to birth, every day, to radiant newness. His word called us, his Spirit was given us and we responded with faith. Now we have to let ourselves be led along the paths of Exodus, the paths of love: "We are to love, then, because he loved us first" (1 Jn 4:19). So we shall now see where the paths of love lead.

CHAPTER FIVE

Exodus, the Paths of Love

When someone opts for freedom, the first thing he feels the need for is to take stock of his situation, to see where he stands in relation to himself and the reality around him. Israel's stock-taking, once the waters of the Sea of Reeds had closed behind them, took the form of a celebration in the Eastern mode: joy takes over, and they sing the event and dance to the rhythm of their song of freedom. As the centuries go by Israel developed and elaborated on the first Song of Moses (Ex 15), and the theme is always the same: "His love is everlasting" (Ps 136). And so for us, too, our pasch is the event of God-with-us, the event of his presence attuned to the song of our true selves, and the theme of our melody is the same: the covenant in his love. This is where we, too, stand in the first movement of our liberation. A Christian is one who, in the risen Christ, has passed through the sea of death because he has been loved with a love that makes him a sharer in the life and freedom of God himself. We come from earth, and the different levels of our being reveal our earthly origins. But we are born, also, to freedom and love: we come from God. To be risen from the dead is to be launched on an orbit that encompasses the whole of reality: God and man, history and the universe, the breadth of human community and the depths of the individual human soul. Our course began with the first gratuitousness of creation and passed through faith in the word of life, whence it flows strongly in ever great freedom.

With this new presence as our starting point, nothing can hold us back from life since our solitude has been shattered by communion, and our dispersion has been gathered up in unity. The unity of communion poured into our hearts by the Spirit must grow and extend its peace to the furthest recesses of our being. This is the long path of Exodus. The word "exodus" means going out, but it is a going out which is spun out in time. The books of Exodus and Numbers tell of the long road from Egypt to Canaan. It is our own paschal journey which is here described: the passage that takes us from the Sea of Reeds—our first liberation—through the waters of the Jordan—our arrival in the land of freedom which is the fullness of God.

THE JOURNEY THROUGH THE DESERT

Whatever human reasons the Israelites may have had for taking the route through the desert instead of taking the shorter path along the coast from Egypt to Canaan (Ex 13:17-21), this period of wandering in the desert has always been seen as specially significant in Israel's encounter with God. In the Bible, the theme of the desert does not have the significance of flight from the world that a later monastic tradition attributes—perhaps too literally—to it. It is, in God's plan for us, a passageway, the path of our pasch leading to a land of liberty where God dwells amongst us. In order to reach this land of the Spirit in which God and man dwell in one another, we must pass through the desolate and inhospitable desert (Dt 1:19). The desert is both a time of trial and of a new love. It is a time in which we learn to be faithful (Dt 8; Hos 2:16-22). The freedom that flows from love and harmony with others is not a handout, we have to respond to it and show that we are free.

God's first objective in leading us through the desert seems to be to enable us to develop the two primary conditions which lie at the heart of the process of liberation: sincerity and a willingness to be saved by him. "Remember how Yahweh your God led you for forty years [the length of a generation] in the wilderness, to humble you, to test you and know your inmost heart" (Dt 8:2). Our journey through life is this journey through the desert, and every stage of it, every circumstance and every being we meet on our way are there to reveal the secret of our inmost heart. Maturity demands that we leave the indecision and fluidity of adolescence behind and take a personal stand which, whether we know it or not, will reveal the truth of ourselves. The humiliation that Deuteronomy speaks of does not have that degrading, negative meaning that we sometimes attribute to it today. It is the "game of truth" that forces us to come down to earth and face up to the truth which is sometimes the farthest from us: ourselves. It is the game of truth of the first years of marriage or—for some of the wiser young couples—of the time of their engagement. Fidelity proves itself through difficulties. The promise hidden in each one of us is revealed when we face up to events. In this sense one can say, with Mounier, "The event is my inner master." Every day of our lives can be seen as a journey through the desert because every day can be the occasion of a genuine act of faith in love and of our budding freedom.

But the long journey through the wilderness is not an examination. It is the revelation of a high presence that tests our capacity for being present to God and to others. The desert is not just the testing-ground of our weakness. It is a new beginning of love, and it transfigures everyday life which we, in our incorrigible lack of realism, think of as a dull routine, empty of all presence. At the time of the first covenant, God told Abraham to walk in his presence and be blameless (Gn 17:1-2), and God only makes himself known to us when we walk with him. This is not just the sign of an active methodology. It also points to a healthy sense of reality which saves us. We are so inclined to seek for God, inner peace and joy outside the concrete circumstances of our lives. No doubt this is why we are always waiting for a better moment to encounter God and set our lives in order. But it is precisely in the source of our daily journey through the desert that we meet God face to face.

The desert is the "open space" into which the Spirit draws us in order to "speak to our hearts" (Hos 2:16). It is the inner destination that prepares us for this meeting (Am 4:12). "Yahweh says this: I remember the affection of your youth, the love of your bridal days: you followed me through the wilderness" (Jer 2:2).

In the desert we come to understand that God trains us, as a man trains his child (Dt 8:6), not brutally and with exterior punishment but by making straight what has been twisted in us. He rectifies the non-realism of our wayward-ness and sets us on the straight path of his presence. He makes us capable of being always present to him, in all sim-plicity, as long as we do not stray away into possessiveness. This straying is always possible, and that is why one of the key words of the journey through the wilderness is *today* (Ps 95:7; Heb 3:7-11).

Today holds the secret of the present moment and of our total presence. God trains us in a sense of reality by teaching us to walk in his presence. "When Israel was a child I loved him, and I called my son out of Egypt. But the more I called to them, the further they went from me. . . . I myself taught Ephraim to walk, I took them in my arms; yet they have not understood that I was the one looking after them" (Hos 11:1-3). When we pray, asking our Father for our bread "today" (Mt 6:11), we are asking for the true manna which our possessive nature would like to store up for the morrow (Ex 16:19-21).

What does this mean, the fact that we are forbidden to store up the bread that nourishes the very substance of our being? It is simply that this bread is someone, the son of God, and no person can be possessed by another. We can only give him a disinterested welcome. "I tell you most solemnly, it was not Moses who gave you bread from heaven, it is my Father who gives you the bread from heaven, the true bread.... I am the bread of life" (Jn 6:32-35). "He fed you with manna which neither you nor your fathers had known, to make you understand that man does not live on bread alone but man lives on everything that comes from the mouth of Yahweh" (Dt 8:3). It is always today when we hear God's voice (Heb 3:7-4:11). His word is not of yesterday nor of tomorrow "the word of our God remains for ever" (Is 40:8), "the Word is very near to you, it is in your mouth and in your heart for your observance" (Dt 30:14). The word of life that we can hear, see with our eyes, contemplate and touch with our hands (1 Jn 1:1-2) is the risen Lord who transfigures our lives today, for "the message of Christ, in all its richness" has its home with us (Col 3:16).

The desert is a spiritual quality in our human life-span, saving us from the deceit of appearance and making us hunger for the essential good: "Set your hearts on his king-dom first, and on his righteousness—which means God him-self and his effective love—and all these other things will be given you as well. So do not worry about tomorrow.... Each day has enough trouble of its own" (Mt 6:33-34). Jesus him-self goes into the desert before beginning the work of estab-lishing the Kingdom, thus fulfilling in his person the time of trial during which Israel often showed itself unfaithful: "Yet I am Yahweh, your God since the days in the land of Egypt; you know no God but me, there is no other savior. I pastured you in the wilderness; in the land of drought I pastured them, and they were satisfied; once satisfied, their hearts grew proud, and so they came to forget me" (Hos 13:4-6). A heart that is satisfied is easily forgetful, whereas a heart that hungers is open to the memory of God and ready to worship. Jesus is tempted first by hunger, but since in him the man is nourished by the Word (Mt 4:4), in the last temptation he can reply in our name to our essential hunger: "You must worship the Lord your God, and serve him alone" (Mt 4:10). We crave for a presence. And the desert of our daily lives sharpens our craving by detaching us from everything that cannot satisfy us. The desert is not a mystique of escape. Far from distracting us from our human task it animates it with an eternal presence without which that task would be a servitude and our "today" a prison.

And so, on the path of our daily life God's pedagogical method is one of presence and it aims at personalizing everything. The typical events which mark the steps of Israel's path through the desert all converge in Christ and reveal God's loving countenance. He gives us *water* and *manna* because he is the loving presence who feeds us and quenches our thirst, "He who comes to me will never be hungry; he who believes in me will never thirst" (Jn 6:35; 4:14). The desert is a battle—against our own lack of faith and the obstacles that stand in the way of our freedom—but the victory comes from him, our pasch and resurrection (Jn 11:25). "I have told you all this so that you may find peace *in me*. In the world you will have trouble, but be brave: I have conquered the world" (Jn 16:33). The term "the world," in the negative sense in which John uses it, has a meaning in relation to mankind somewhat similar to that of "the body," in relation to the individual, in Paul's thought. It is the "unspiritual" still divorced from love. And just as, on the personal level, peace unifies our being in the assurance of being loved so, on the community level, peace is the victory of faith. "Anyone who has been begotten by God has already overcome the world: this is the victory over the world—our faith" (1 Jn 5:4).

This same path leading to the light of God's countenance can be traced in other themes of the journey through the desert. The *road* that we follow is not just the result of various pre-determined factors, nor is it the ideal of our moral imperatives. We only become free if we walk with someone and in him: "I am the Way . . . follow me" (Jn 14:6; Mt 9:9). And it is always today since Christ is risen: "Jesus himself came up and walked by their side" (Lk 24:15). God is our guide during this long journey out of bondage, and he walks by our side under the guise of the *shepherd* and of the *cloud*. His presence is very real. He is not with us as someone "on the outside" but as an inner presence, transforming us into himself. We become what we gaze upon: "He lived among us, and we saw his glory" (Jn 1:14). This is what loving means, to become the beloved by entering into his joy (Mt 25:21). The Book of Numbers, by describing the journey through the desert as a series of *stages*, is describing our journey in Christ. In him we go "from beginning to beginning toward beginnings that will have no end" (Gregory of Nyssa). The Bible is the story of God's journey and man's toward their face to face encounter. It is the story of Christ's journey in us, of ours in him, not in nostalgic memories but in an ever fuller and transforming presence: "All I want is to know Christ and the power of his Resurrection and to share his sufferings by reproducing the pattern of his death. That is the way I can hope to take my place in the resurrection of the dead. Not that I have become perfect yet: I have not yet won, but I am still running, trying to capture the prize for which Christ

Jesus captured me . . . I forget the past and I strain ahead for what is still to come" (Phil 3:10-13).

THE PATHS OF THE LAW

In too many lives the process of liberation comes to nothing. Too many Christians have abandoned the struggle through discouragement or have been side-tracked into the closed circuit of moralism or the unreal paths of a spirituality cut off from life. A Christian must go through the experience of the desert if his total personality is to take shape and reach spiritual fulfillment. The biblical image of the desert as the time of betrothal is astonishingly full of truth. What happens to an engaged couple? They are a world unto themselves, and everything revolves around the center of their reality. But this stage is temporary; life sees to it that they be called to greater maturity. However, the stage of being alone with each other is necessary for them if they are to open up their lives each to the other. And it is equally necessary that we experience the desert as a spiritual zone in life in which God and each human being are a world apart. In the desert they get to know each other, they can speak heart to heart, for only the heart which loves can really know another.

Our journey through the desert is our daily journey through life. It is a time of dialogue and of discovery of another person, preparing us for the fullness of presence. Of course, certain periods seem more intensely filled with presence than others, according to the rhythm of our work and leisure, but gradually the whole of our day comes to be lit with God's presence. And so we can see how the experience of the desert is a prolongation of the experience of creation.

Time, which appears as the measuring rod of our daily growing and which we were inclined to waste in the early period
of anarchy or attempt to hold on to, is seen in fact to be a free
gift of presence. We cannot welcome it unless we are present
to what it holds for us in an attitude of poverty. And this is the
lesson of the desert: it calls us to return to our original purity
of heart in which we can, once again, be present to gratuitousness.

God has not created two kinds of humanity: an "average" mass of men condemned to remain in bondage, and a
select few who could escape through the desert. This escape
route is a necessary condition for every human being to grow
in his divinized human condition. It is the way that every man
must take to be acclimated to freedom, to become acquainted
with the divine mentality and prepare himself for interior
unity and union with others. But, in the desert, there are
some paths that should be followed and others to be avoided
in order to reach our goal of freedom. It is vital to take correct bearings, as the right paths lead to life; all others to
death. God's method of teaching his people in the desert was
shown in a central event: the gift of the law. In general the law
is a norm for life, guidelines that permit our personal
dynamic to run its full course while respecting our own true
welfare and that of others. It is all-important that we understand the value and limits of the law in life.

The true paths which God teaches us to follow in the
desert are the paths of our own hearts leading us to him (Hos
11:3-4). There is an essential link between our own rectitude
of heart and his presence, between the law of Moses, the law
of the gospel, or the natural law (Rom 2:12-15), must, first and

foremost, be understood as a gift from God and a call to him. It is remarkable that the basis of the law given to Moses, the Ten Commandments—both in the texts of sacerdotal tradition (Ex 20:1-17) and in those of Deuteronomy (Dt 5:6-21)— is not expressed as an impersonal code but as a dialogue: "Listen, Israel" (Dt 5:1; 6:4). Its focal point is immediately explicit: it is God, the love that saves. "I am Yahweh your God who brought you out of the land of Egypt, out of the house of slavery" (Ex 20:2; Dt 5:6). This is the central fact around which everything that follows revolves. Even by comparison with the precepts of the natural law or of contemporary Eastern legal codes, the atmosphere that permeates the Decalogue is absolutely novel. Already it is the atmosphere of love that the gospel later comes to accomplish (Mt 5:7). "Listen, Israel: Yahweh our God is the one Yahweh. You shall love Yahweh your God with all your heart, with all your soul, with all your strength. Let these words I urge on you today be written on your heart" (Dt 6:4-6).

The function of law in our lives is, essentially, in relation to the heart. "Until today Yahweh has given you no heart to understand, no eyes to see, no ears to hear. For forty years I led you to the wilderness...learning thus that I, Yahweh, am your God" (Dt 29:4). As the desert is the spiritual time of preparation that accustoms us to his presence, so the heart is the spiritual place in which the encounter takes place. We have to seek him with all our hearts (Dt 4:29) and return to him with all our hearts (1 Sm 7:3). To let the words of the law be written on our hearts (Dt 6:6) is to welcome the lawgiver. And so, while we are still on our way to the land of freedom, our hearts are the dwelling-place of him who is going before us, leading us to freedom. "What house could you build me, what place could you make for my rest? My eyes are drawn to the man of humbled and contrite spirit" (Is 66:1-2). Later, when Jesus, risen from the dead, joins the disciples on their way and explains how he is personally present in the law and the Prophets, they experience the truth of these words in their own burning hearts: "Did not our hearts burn within us as he talked to us on the road and explained the scriptures to us?" (Lk 24:32).

God gives us a law, a way of life, so that his word can accompany us along that way and dwell in us. In the light of his presence we can see the place that Paul attributes to the law with relation to the fullness of Christ (Gal 4:1-6): it is a teacher that forms our conscience by telling us what is sinful (Rom 3:20). If we remember that the first condition for becoming free is to recognize that we are held in captivity, then we can see that this function of the law is indispensable to our freedom. It cannot, of itself, set us free, any more than a signpost can assist us along the road it points to, but it is a necessary preparation for freedom. The law exists in relation to sin: "The Law is sacred.... I should not have known what sin was except for the Law" (Rom 7:12, 7). It has been given to us because of sin and so that we may be conscious of it (Gal 3:19). Our impatience to reach a state of autonomy in which the rules of life coincide with our own spontaneous movements often leads us—especially nowadays—to neglect the preliminary condition for reaching this happy state: the recognition of what we have to free ourselves from by humbly acknowledging that we are under the sway of other laws. If we look at the incoherent state of Israel's moral conscience in the light of the various legal codes promulgated throughout its history, we can recognize something akin to our own incoherence. Many groups and individuals in the world, whatever may be their cultural sophistication, need to learn the rudiments of the Mosaic law. Its moral precepts are not abolished but accomplished by the love of the gospel.

We must not be put off by the first peremptory and negative impression of the law. Any educator knows that if he has no authority he can have no tenderness either. On the other hand, a negative law points clearly to the path that must be followed by an unformed conscience. When parents leave their children alone in the house for a few hours, they do not tell them in general, positive terms to take good care of everything. They tell them not to turn on the gas or to throw things out of the windows. The apparently negative approach of the law is not contrary to the open initiative of charity. It is the first step in its realization. For egoists, such as we are, to be formed in charity it is never superfluous for us to be reminded of the minimum demands of justice. "If you love your fellow men you have carried out your obligations" (Rom 13:9). Charity goes even farther since it consists in loving as Christ loved (Jn 15:12), but it must begin with the first steps of the law.

However, once we have recognized the necessary and positive function of law, we must also recognize its limits. The imperfection inherent in the law is not a question of formulation. The law of Moses is still valid and relevant in regard to our interior anarchy. The limits of the law are of another order and, in this sense, are the same for all law whether it be evangelical or Mosaic, natural or positive. The fundamental failure of law is that it is radically powerless to set us free. We can follow its precepts; in fact, it is indispensable that we do so, but law, as such, will always be a norm that remains extraneous to our personal life-thrust. "All that law does is to tell us what is sinful" and to be avoided, or what is good and should be sought after (Rom 3:20). It can never give the strength to accomplish what it teaches. The merit of the law lies in the light it sheds; its inherent powerlessness in the fact that it is not love. Only the advent of a new source of energy can give us the power to resolve this contradiction, and that is the absolute newness of the New Law, the gift of the Holy Spirit who becomes the life principle within us (Rom 8:1-4). In him we are no longer heteronomous but autonomous.

Once we understand this, we are freed for a further spiritual growth. A study of religions—not excluding certain forms of Christianity—would prove this by a counter-proof: a religion becomes fossilized once its mystical impulse is codified into an ethic. Many factors contribute to this slow death, and two are especially evident: sociological pressures and the impersonal ethic of the super-ego. For many people, religion is the result of the imperatives imposed by these two blind forces: the social entity and the irrational moral conscience. Not that we can entirely discount these factors, but at least we should see them for what they are and no more. The jewel-box is not the jewel. Certain means of locomotion may be necessary for a forward movement; they do not necessarily give the illusion that they can supply the motor power. And since it is a question of man's liberation, we must take care not to confuse our own polluted atmosphere with the breath of God. If we wish to keep legal values where they belong and delve further into the true sources of our autonomy as sons of God, we must be aware of the dangers of paralysis from legalism.

Here we come back to the "game of truth" of our first paschal liberation, and it leads us this time to a harrowing revision of values such as is dramatically illustrated in the life of one of the greatest Christian spirits of all time: St. Paul. This totalitarian Pharisee, who had put all his faith in a generous and heroic observance of the law, discovered as a consequence of his own fidelity that the law cannot give life. He learned that the true, liberating function of the law is to open our hearts to the living God who alone can save us. The radical powerlessness of the law—of any law including our own generous resolutions or our careful programs for perfection—makes us more sensitive to the invitation to allow ourselves to be saved by grace. The complexities of law make us long for the pure space of gratuitousness in which we can breathe freely. We can all honestly say that we have experienced the failure of any law in our lives to restore and heal us from within. If we allow the light of a humble sense of reality to fall upon the death-instinct concealed in our social "persona" or in the blind super-ego, then the depths of our being can open up to the personal presence that alone is capable of bringing us to life. Humility is the only "law" capable of penetrating our psychological defenses and of opening us to God within us, to Christ our Savior. We cannot be made "righteous" or "justified" if we continue to pride ourselves on our illusions of fidelity to the law, like the Pharisee in the Gospel, but only if we recognize that life springs from the heart and first of all from the heart of him who loves us: "God, be merciful to me, a sinner" (Lk 18:9-14). The paths of the law are the paths of life not because they give life but because they lead to God, the source of life.

THE SPIRIT OF FREEDOM

"God's justice that was made known through the law and the Prophets has now been revealed outside the law, since it is the same justice of God that comes through faith to everyone, Jew and Pagan alike, who believes in Jesus Christ" (Rom 3:21-22). Our justification, the deep and essential "rectification" we need, can never be a work of our own organizing. We cannot attain inner balance by planning for it. We are not inanimate things, and we cannot reach perfection by skillful manipulation of our mechanism. We are persons, nuclei of communion with others. Our liberation can be achieved only on this level. But we have seen that faith is the initial opening of our personal mystery toward others. A certain liberation is achieved through communion with other human beings, but it cannot be complete for they, like ourselves, struggle in the bonds of loneliness and inner chaos. Our essential liberation can only be reached by opening toward someone who is in essence free and "just." It is because God is "just," because he is free and totally without subterfuge or pretense that he can justify and rectify us and set us free. God is just, and he justifies everyone who believes in Jesus (Rom 3:26). Christ is the manifestation of God-Love (Ti 3:4-7). By belief in him we enter into a world of personal gratuitousness, we become free.

"If any man is thirsty, let him come to me! Let the man come and drink who believes in me" (Jn 7:37-38). In the Bible, water is the symbol of grace: "All who want it may have the water of life, and have it free" (Rv 22:17; Is 55:1). But the grace that is offered is someone: "He was speaking of the Spirit which those who believed in him were to receive; for there was no Spirit as yet because Jesus had not yet been glorified"—that is to say crucified and raised from the dead (Jn 7:39). In the definitive step he took beyond death, Christ became the "life-giving spirit" (1 Cor 15:45). The Spirit, grace in person, is the Spirit of the risen Lord. In his rising from the dead, Christ brought man's nature into the realm of true life. In his gift to us of the Spirit, he gives each one of us the possibility of personally attaining to this true life of freedom. "Where the Spirit of the Lord is, there is freedom" (2 Cor 3:17). By baptism we are plunged into Christ's resurrection (Rom 6:1-10), we all drink of the same Spirit (1 Cor 12:13). "Anyone who is joined to the Lord is one spirit with him" (1 Cor 6:17). When we welcomed the law in to our hearts, we became the dwelling place of God's word and dwelt in him (Jn 8:31-32). When we come to drink of his Spirit we taste freedom. Throughout our daily journeying our inner division can now be resolved in unity. The "flesh" can be unified in the dynamic flow of the Spirit: "Your interests, however, are not in the unspiritual, but in the spiritual, since the Spirit of God has made his home in you" (Rom 8:9).

When a psychologist describes the path of inner liberation as a passage from instinct to the spirit, it is a perfect expression of what takes place. But it is important to understand that it is a question, essentially, of a personal experience of the living Spirit. It is not simply an impersonal idealism or an abstract experience of "soul." It is the existential experience of the Spirit of the risen Christ who proceeds from the Father. "If the Spirit of him who raised Jesus from the dead is living in you, then he who raised Jesus from the dead will give life to your own mortal bodies through his Spirit living in you" (Rom 8:11). A sense of reality such as this is enough to give integral direction to our work of personal fulfillment, for in seeking our own liberation we are not simply seeking a moral perfection, but we are laying the groundwork for our total liberation, body, soul and spirit. "May the God of peace make you perfect and holy; and may you all be kept safe and blameless, spirit, soul and body, for the coming of our Lord Jesus Christ. God has called you and he will not fail you" (1 Thes 5:23-24).

What are the signs by which we recognize the perfect peace in which we find liberation? We know that it is an accomplishment. "The Law was given through Moses, grace and truth have come through Jesus Christ" (Jn 1:17). On Sinai, Moses gave the people the norms of life to be followed by the lower levels of our personality. From a purely empirical point of view most people now agree that on each level of our being there are certain self-regulating laws for the protection of life, and when we ignore them, they set off danger signals such as sickness, anxiety, guilt neuroses and so on. But the real problem is the convergence and unification of the various levels of being. A unity and peace that reach into all levels must come from the highest level. "Since you have been brought back to true life with Christ, you must look for the things that are in heaven, where Christ is" (Col 3:1). The Spirit is the peak of our being and our unification must necessarily lie along the axis of the dynamic of the Spirit. The Spirit of Love is in person the fulfillment of our own inner thrust.

On the new Sinai of the Beatitudes (Mt 5:17), Jesus reveals the accomplishment of the law. An accomplishment must necessarily be a continuation of what it comes to accomplish, but at the same time it must contribute something completely original. The Spirit is this accomplishment, crowning the continuity of our beings from the biological to the social and from the deepest unconscious to the highest lucidity of consciousness. But he can only be the crowning point of our inherent gifts because he is radically new. This newness does not consist in a more perfect synthesis of the law but in the fact that the Spirit, instead of being an exterior norm, becomes our interior life-principle: the accomplishment of all our potentialities is in a person. "The water that I shall give will turn into a spring inside him, welling up to eternal life" (Jn 4:14). And this is the beatitude. All our lofty principles leave us dying of thirst. Only a personal presence can satisfy us.

This presence is divine. It does not thrust aside any part of our true self. Like the burning bush, we burn but are not consumed. The Spirit in us has infinite respect for what we are; that is why he can be within us in a unique transcendence and yet with an immanence that no human person could attain. The Spirit becomes the source as we ourselves become source of our own personality. This is the true autonomy of freedom. As long as we are imprisoned behind the walls of our own self-sufficiency we are not autonomous, we are slaves of our own self-idolatry. We only become free and autonomous when we open up in a communion. But other human beings with whom we try desperately to establish a liberating communion are slaves, just as we are. If we hope to quench the essential thirst of our being in them, we shall only be digging "leaky cisterns that hold no water" (Jer 2:13). But if we accept the true "fountain of living water" (Jer 2:13; Jn 4:14) within us, not only shall we attain our own full freedom, but we shall also become capable of a tireless and life-giving communion with all human beings.

The New Testament speaks of a new law, therefore, and we must understand that it is a totally new way of life because it is a person, a life-giving presence. Christian maturity is forged in the desert, and on our path through the desert this presence is the only spring that can quench our thirst and that will never run dry. It becomes our most vital inner instinct: "Deep within them I will plant my Law, writing it on their hearts" (Jer 31:33). "I shall give you a new heart, and put a new spirit in you; I shall remove the heart of stone from your bodies and give you a heart of flesh instead" (Ez 36:26). The spontaneity of love is our true autonomy. As long as we still do what is good because it is commanded and avoid doing evil because it is forbidden, we are not free, we are still subject to a law that is exterior to ourselves. We only become free in fact when we do good because we love the good and we avoid evil because we hate it. "Since the Spirit is our life, let us be directed by the Spirit" (Gal 5:25).

It is quite obvious that such freedom is not improvised overnight. Peace is the fruit of a struggle: "You cannot belong to Christ Jesus unless you crucify all self-indulgent passions and desires" (Gal 5:24), not by inhibiting them but by assuming them onto a higher level. In fact only love is capable of assuming and fulfilling the demands of life which burst out on every level. Spiritual freedom has nothing to do with license: that would be simply falling back into a bondage rationalized by a pretended sublimation. "My brothers, you were called as you know, to liberty; but be careful, or this liberty will provide an opening for self-indulgence" (Gal 5:13). The sign of an authentic liberty is peace within oneself and with others in a self-sharing of one's whole being. The goal of the first Passover was to "offer worship to God on this mountain" (Ex 3:12). Our own liberty, won at great cost in the desert, reaches its goal on the Mount of the Beatitudes in a gesture of service, a disinterested outgoing toward others. Later we shall see how that wonderfully human love is God's sublime liturgy.

Paul courageously affirms that in the realm of the Spirit there is no more law. Since it stands in relation to sin and death, we are freed from the law when we are freed from sin and death. As long as we remember by what paths we attain to the spiritual freedom that is love, it is true that once we reach the mountain top there are no more paths. A nurse leaves the hospital when her working hours are done, whatever may be the condition of her patients. She has "done her duty," and it is in order for her to go. A mother who is nursing her sick child does not need prescribed working hours; her "duty" will be done only when her child is better. She is free of the law. "What the Spirit brings is very different: love, joy, peace, patience, kindness, goodness, trustfulness, gentleness and self-control. There can be no law against things like that, of course" (Gal 5:22-23). It is obvious that our inner unity is hardly won and that we can never rest on our laurels. At the peak of our being, breathing the pure air of grace and of life, there can be no room for grasping possessiveness, for feeling that we are entitled to ease or privilege. He who is faithful has called us to an adventure in the Spirit, and we have never "done our duty" by love. We must go on from one discovery to another. If we look back, we can see that "we are rid of the Law, freed by death from our imprisonment free to *serve* in the new spiritual way and not the old way of a written law" (Rom 7:6). If we consent to prune off the dead wood that weighs us down, our exodus can become an ever-new way of love: if the source springs within us, youth is always ahead.

CHAPTER SIX

The Covenant, the Depths of Love

Once we reach spiritual freedom we reach a point of unity which allows us to live the fullness of our total human experience. To borrow the language of St. Paul, let us now attempt to measure its breadth and its depth (Eph 3:18-20). Once again we can see the path we follow illustrated in the story of God's people in the Old Testament. The phase of the covenant enacted on Sinai ushers us into the depths of love. The phase of the kingdom, established when the Israelites settled in the promised land, will be our introduction into the breadth of the mystery of charity.

The preceding phases of our human pasch have convinced us of at least one invariable in our life, and that is that God is not to be sought outside our daily experience. He reveals himself to us within the flow of our trend toward liberation. Matter is energy waiting to be liberated. Is energy the spirit waiting to be liberated? Whatever it may be, the spirit is the energy of love which tends toward the liberation of all things in the gratuitousness of a personalized universe. The phase of the promise is the first appearance of gratuitousness in person on the scene of man's adventure. The first pasch and the first Exodus are the further development of the divine energy at work in man and through man. When man reaches true freedom of the Spirit, even if only in flashes, the presence that he received with life and that has accompanied him along his way reveals and gives itself to him in a new and more personal light.

In our original darkness we were incapable of seeing and loving God as he really is. But that is precisely what will be demanded of us in the world of gratuitousness. God is the birth of a new life within us. He is our freedom and our path to freedom. But who is this mysterious presence within us that completely gratifies and gladdens us in an inexhaustible communion? "You have made us for yourself, O God," but who are you? "I beg you, tell me your name," asked Jacob after his long struggle in the dark with the angel, and the angel only revealed to him his own name: Israel (Gn 32:29-30). On Sinai, when the Lord said, "I know you by name," Moses begged, "let me see your glory" (Ex 33:12-18). And the apostles, when they had understood that Jesus was the true way, asked him, "Lord, let us see the Father and then we shall be satisfied" (Jn 14:5-8). Can we know God?

GRACE OR GRATUITOUSNESS IN PERSON

If we want to find God, we must consent to live in gratuitousness. At every stage of our liberation we have seen that this is where our life-force lies: gratuitousness is buried like a seed within the first creation. In the first awakening to freedom it is there as the free response of faith. In our first effective liberation it is there to unify our being. In our journey in the desert we have seen it as the personal presence which fills our every need. The covenant of Sinai, in conformity with the teaching function of the law, is a temporary, historical "disposition" which in no way invalidates the original disposition of the promise which is wholly gratuitous (Gal 3:17-18). The true and final disposition is the new covenant in the Spirit (2 Cor 3:6) which establishes us in the freedom of sons (Gal 4:5). Our human condition is not governed by the letter of the law. Its movements cannot be calculated in advance: the Spirit breathes where he wills, when he wills and as he wills. Often we misunderstand the spiritual teachers on this score as though they taught a fatalist doctrine of resignation, since God gives himself as and when he wishes. But Paul warns us against bitterness: "Does it follow that God is unjust? Of course not.... The only thing that counts is not what human beings want or try to do, but the mercy of God." And so there is "no distinction between Jew and Greek: all belong to the same Lord who is rich enough, however many ask his help" (Rom 9:14-18; 10:12).

The fact is that God *always* wants to give himself. He is always present. But as his presence is essentially a free presence of grace, it is we who have to ask ourselves: are we open and available to grace? Are we tuned in to his wavelength or are we searching for ourselves elsewhere? Are we living in the full light of our destitution which makes us open to the light of his mercy? There is nothing degrading in doing so since our human condition is precisely one of servitude as long as we remain in the prison of our solitude. To see ourselves in the depths of our destitution is not a passive but an eminently active point of view. We are never so truly ourselves as when we become receptive to God, mustering the whole of our being in the act of giving him welcome. A long road and a hard struggle go before the attainment of the true Mount Sinai and the vision of God's glory (Lk 9:28-35; Ex 33:18-34:9; 1 Kgs 19:9-14). On the other hand this activity is not activism. To want to die to our own egotistical anarchy is a path to life only if it orients all our activity toward God and others. Spiritual activism consists in relying upon one's own efforts, and it is this that Paul condemns when he says that it is not "what human beings want or try to do" that counts (Rom 9:14). Our ultimate liberation is to open ourselves to a new presence, and the peak of our activity, therefore, is to relax in the gratuitousness of receiving. The more he frees us the more he gives himself. His gift is a presence of light. Our task is to open the blinds of our prison and let in the rays of his light.

It is a wonderful thing to realize that the covenant, by which God gives himself in person to his people and which was to reach fulfillment in the promised land, was actually contracted quite unpredictably in the middle of the wilderness. In this wild country a mountain rears its head and God gives himself there. In that barren land "Israel was sacred to Yahweh" (Jer 2:2-3). The reciprocal belonging in love, when he gives himself to us and we to him, is always an unpredictable, spontaneous event from which flows life.

"Moses then went up to God. . . . Yahweh came down on the mountain...and Moses went up" (Ex 19:3-20). These human images indicate what takes place in our meeting with

God. In order to be raised up, one must be lowered, says the Gospel. In order to be caught up in loving grace we must hide in the crevice of Christ, our rock. This is the "state of grace" in which our being is unified. Here God can seize us (Phil 3:12) and carry us on "eagle's wings" (Ex 19:4; Dt 32:11). The humility that places us squarely on the solid ground of our human condition is truly "theological," for it ensures our contact with the rock of God's wondrous presence. To see his face we must revert constantly to poverty of heart. "I bless you, Father, Lord of heaven and of earth, for hiding these things from the learned and the clever and revealing them to mere children…no one knows who the Father is except the Son and those to whom the Son chooses to reveal him" (Lk 10:21-22). "My spirit exults in God my savior; because he has looked upon his lowly hand-maid" (Lk 1:47-48). "My eyes are drawn to the man of humbled and contrite spirit" (Is 66:2). When we are really present in the depths of our heart, God cannot resist us. So in the state of grace we are ourselves and his presence can fill us with a light that darkness cannot overpower (Jn 1:5).

But humility is transparent to the light of God only because it is a view of faith. Moses goes up into a thick cloud (Ex 19:9-16), and our faith is like the eyes of love that pierce the cloud of darkness. To believe in Christ is to open the eyes of our heart (Eph 1:18) "until the dawn comes and the morning star rises in your minds" (2 Pt 1:19). We are in his hands. However obscure things may seem, why should we be afraid? The state of grace is a state of assurance, of the assurance that we are loved. God gives himself to us as the sun gives its light. And just as trust is a necessary corollary to human love, hope is necessary to our living experience of God, the fullness of love. In hope, our hearts can prepare a dwelling for the grace of his presence.

THROUGH THE SON

"No one can come to me unless he is drawn by the Father who sent me.... No one can come to the Father except through me" (Jn 6:44; 14:6). Ultimately, gratuitousness is our deepest hunger because it is a person who draws us to himself. Beginning with Sinai, the Old Testament expressed this mysterious attraction in the theme of the mountain which brings earth closer to heaven. "Oh, that you would tear the heavens open and come down—at your Presence the mountains would melt" (Is 64:1). In the Gospel we read of seven mountains on which Christ shows himself to be the personal fulfillment of the age-old longings of the poor. On the mountain of the Temptation the trials of the desert culminate in the new temple in which God is worshipped in spirit and in truth (Ex 20; Mt 4:1-11; Jn 4:19-24). On the mountain of the Beatitudes the law bursts like a ripe fruit, scattering the new life of grace and truth (Ex 20; Mt 5–7). On the mountain where Jesus multiplied the loaves the true manna sent by the Father and the banquet of the covenant are already present (Ex 24; Jn 6). On the mountain of the Transfiguration, God's love shines, like a radiant light, on the face of Christ (Ex 34; Lk 9:28-36). On the mountain of the Agony, the intercession of the new Moses is victorious over the abandonment of God's people (Ex 32–33; Lk 22:39-46). On Calvary the new and eternal covenant is sealed in the blood of the Lamb (Ex 24; Lk 22-23). Finally, on the mountain of the Ascension men who are now free are drawn toward the intimacy of the Father (Ex 33:12-23; Lk 24:50-51; Eph 4:8-10).

In the fullness of grace of the new universe the true mountain of the covenant will be the mountain of the new Jerusalem (Jn 4:20-24; Is 2:1-5; 4:4-6; 25). But now the power of attraction, drawing us to God's fullness, passes through Christ crucified and risen again. "And when I am lifted up from the earth, I shall draw all men to myself" (Jn 12:32). Our experience of the God of love is the experience of all things recapitulated in the son (Eph 1:10). "The Son of Man must be lifted up . . . so that everyone who believes may have eternal life in him" (Jn 3:14). If through faith we are really consumed with passion for him, then a new life overflows, capturing all the seeds of death in us.

Our "access" to God is Jesus lived by us personally (Eph 2:18; Heb 10:19). It is distressing to see how many Christians live with only a vague notion of "Almighty God" and that the countenance of the Father is quite unknown to them. Our relationship with God is not a direct line from us to the Father in a disembodied individualism. It goes through his "well-beloved Son" (Lk 9:35; 3:22). In fact it is the movement of the son toward his Father which has become ours, since Christ is the living movement of God in our lives, traveling our road with us and sharing our human condition. It is vital that we establish our foundations in him (Col 2:6-7). We have seen that the need for gratuitousness in the process of our liberation constantly brings us back to an attitude of humility: this is what it means to revert constantly to Christ. He is God, present in all truth on the deepest level both of our destitution and of our greatest potential. The truth that sets us free is not a question of moral therapy, it is personal communion with the son, he who is supremely free (Jn 8:35) and who is within us even in the depths of our deepest bondage. "There is no other savior but me," insists Isaiah; "For of all the names in the world given to men, this is the only one by which we can be saved," declares Peter who feels himself bound to proclaim what he has seen and heard (Acts 4:12-20). Peter knows, and so do we, that since Christ's resurrection the depths of God's love have been given to us in Jesus: "To have seen me is to have seen the Father" (Jn 14:9).

IN THE SPIRIT

And yet it is sadly true that for many Christians, Christ does not in fact reveal the Father. Could this be because, to all intents and purposes, they do not recognize the gift of the Spirit in their lives? For without him it is not possible to "see" the living Christ, and consequently it is not possible to see the Father. "I shall ask the Father and he will give you another Advocate to be with you for ever.... On that day you will understand that I am in my Father and you in me and I in you" (Jn 14:16-20).

It is not enough for us to know in theory that the Spirit has been given us. At this stage of our personal history more than at any other, God cannot be known as an object. He is someone by whom we live, and we can only know him by living in him. We can only breathe the breath of the Spirit if we are free. Love is the road that we must follow in order to recognize him who lives in us and whom we have hitherto ignored. And this road passes necessarily through the narrow "gate" of the crucified Christ. The roads of the law are a daily reminder of this.

It is indispensable that we be interiorly relaxed if we are ever to discover that the spiritual environment in which we live and move is a personal presence. It is the Spirit. It can take us years to find out that the medium of our lives is, actually and in all reality, a person. And many Christians go in ignorance of this, in spite of a generous self-giving and devotion to Christ, because they give themselves in a way that is exterior and inspired by activism. They try to force the Spirit to play the game of their own natural reactions, mistaking the exercise of their natural powers with the gentle and forceful unfolding of divine energy. Their lack of interior depth makes it impossible for them to be rectified and made flexible in depth by the divine action that Paul calls ("the Law of the Spirit" [Rom 8:2]). The Spirit cannot be described from an exterior viewpoint since he is pure interiority, and that is why someone who is not sufficiently interiorly purified cannot perceive him. The closer one gets to God the less complicated one becomes; but one must be simple and uncomplicated for God to come close. This is what the covenant actually effects: reciprocity in love.

All this should not discourage us from seeking to deepen the experience of love. On the contrary, we have to be aware of this in order to acquire the habit of a greater soberness of heart. The things of the Spirit cannot be treated as mental concepts nor as empirical methods of action. Above all they must not be confused with the feeling of enthusiasm we experience when our intelligence has seized upon their nature, a feeling which remains powerless to effect any true change in us. Far from discouraging us, the fact that the experience of the Spirit is bound up with our fundamental liberation can be a strong stimulus to us to open ourselves to his action. This is the "theological sense of humor" in faith that guarantees our honesty in the different phases of our pasch. For every time we come up against an aspect of our interior bondage, whether it be new or already well known to us, we have to open ourselves to him who is our free environment, just as the dew does not hide from the rays of the sun but allows itself to be absorbed by them. Love feeds on these small signs, and the freedom of our love is strengthened by many minor liberations throughout our days. If we remain alone with our inner conflicts, we can, at best, analyze our state of mind, diagnose the cause of our difficulties and decide upon a course of treatment. But we remain on the level of the law and of exterior means. Only if we open ourselves in humility to the Spirit who knows the inner secrets of God's nature (1 Cor 2:10-11), can we receive within ourselves the spontaneity of love. In the light of a beloved presence all shadows and conflicts are effaced; without this presence it is virtually impossible to restore the flow of communion in which we find freedom.

And the Spirit is a ceaseless presence of light and love within us. Every time we consent to simplicity before him we can experience that he is the Spirit of the risen Christ. This means that although servitude is a fundamental aspect of our human condition, the fact that we are risen is another and is indeed the most authentic aspect. In the humble experience of the Spirit we pass from decay to youth. Jesus risen from the dead is the firstfruits of the new creation; the Spirit who dwells in us is the full harvest. This is the meaning of the continuous Pentecost into which our baptism introduced us. But we must understand that the experience of the Spirit is not the elation of a solitary prayer but the very stuff of our daily joys and tragedies. Some books of piety would have us think that only a few great and privileged souls can experience a truly personal life in the Spirit. But, as we said before, there are not two types of humanity. We all have to live in the details of day-to-day life. The wonderful work of the Spirit—proclaimed by the apostles, in many languages, on the first morning of Pentecost—is that he is given day by day to all men who consent to be poor enough to recognize him. "How happy are the poor in spirit; theirs is the kingdom of heaven" (Mt 5:3).

If we understand this about the reality of the Spirit—lived from within as the life-breath of man and the transcendental mystery of God—then we can understand the wonderful works of the Spirit who is joined to our spirit to make it divine (Rom 8:14-16). Our new life in the risen Christ (1 Cor 1:30; Rom 8:1) is to live in the Spirit (Rom 8:5). He, personally, is our existential environment, and this is why all the coordinates of our life come together in him in a fullness of personal being which is both his and ours. No movement of our renewed being (Eph 4:23) is foreign to him. In the Bible the Spirit never appears in human form—this is reserved to the incarnate word—because he is the source and origin of all human form (Jn 4:14). There is a certain analogy between the role of the Spirit and the role of the mother in the making of a man. But the specific function of the Spirit is not only to form us in the likeness of Christ (Rom 8:29) and to bring us to birth in him (Jn 3:5), it is also to lead us from within to our eternal maturity. By leading us to "the complete truth" (Jn 16:13), he leads us to full stature in Christ, truth in person (Jn 14:6; Eph 4:13). Our deepest aspiration is to become "living men," and the Spirit is the fruitful plentitude within us that enables us to become fully ourselves.

The Spirit is all of love, in person. Our inner being is fulfilled and set free in him because he is the New Law written in our hearts. In him all things take on personal features: all men can reveal their true features because Christ's features are mirrored in theirs and the distant God comes close. In Christ's face we see the face of the Father. Without this experience of the Spirit, the risen Jesus would simply be nothing more than an ideal of the past, men would be incorrigibly separated from each other and God would be banished to the realms of metaphysics or legalism. We said when we reach spiritual freedom, we reach the point of convergence of all aspects of our human experience. Our intuition of this truth is confirmed when we realize that the point of convergence is someone, the Spirit, and that the mystery of his person lies beyond the grasp of our own psychology. We fulfill ourselves in him because he draws us out of ourselves in a wonderfully fulfilling "otherness" not only in God our Father, but also in every human being, our brother, in every material thing that can become an object of love, in every moment of time that becomes our opportunity to give welcome to love.

In this light we can read all that the New Testament tells us of the "Good News" as an experience of power and of the Spirit, of joy and of the Spirit, of peace and of the Spirit. If we read it in the light of what we have just seen, we shall be in no danger of neglecting our human experience. On the contrary, we can come back to it with a truer sense of its reality and in greater depth. The "brightness of the Lord" becomes ours in the Spirit and transfigures us (2 Cor 3:13 f). He dwells in us (Rom 8:11), makes of each one of us a temple of God (1 Cor 6:19) and of all of us together a new Body (1 Cor 12), a new dwelling-place of the Spirit (Eph 2:22), the Church. But before divine charity can flow untrammeled in men, they have to be plunged into the depths of the Spirit within them. He is our way toward the Father.

TOWARD THE FATHER

"My desire has been crucified and there is not in me any sensuous fire, but living water bounding up in me, and saying inside me, 'Come to the Father'" (Ignatius of Antioch, Letter to the Romans, 7). The testimony of Ignatius could be echoed by any Christian who lives by the Spirit, the "spring inside him, welling up to eternal life" (Jn 4:14). "And eternal life is this: to know you, the only true God" (Jn 17:3). Do we really know God our Father? Who is this God we live with?

There are two barriers that often stand between us and the Father. The first is within ourselves. When the Church transmits the word of God concerning the mystery of the Father, we are necessarily influenced in our way of hearing this message by our own experience of paternity in our father. Modern psychology makes it very clear that this first experience conditions all subsequent relations with authority. To the extent to which we have failed to integrate our first experience in this respect harmoniously and naturally, our fundamental relations with God may also be distorted. Some people have a permanently infantile relationship with God, and Marxist critics are right in seeing an expression of this in many types of religious behavior. Others reject and "murder" their father, and some forms of atheism or of loss of faith seem to stem from this. When a person is about thirty years old and reaches a certain level of social emancipation he may well believe that he can free himself from God. In fact he may simply be freeing himself from the ascendancy of his parents. The work of the Spirit is to heal these first wounds with infinite patience and to cleanse our relations with the Father of all human failings. But one can see the tremendous responsibility of parents who, whether they intend it or not, convey an image of God to their children.

The second barrier to a clear vision of the Father is erected by other Christians and by the way in which they present the mystery of our Father in heaven. Too many Christians retain a vague mental image of God as the old man with a beard who floats above the clouds. Daniel speaks of "The Ancient of Days" and gives a wholly anthropomorphic description (Dn 7), but he does not portray an "old man." The Ancient is one whom time cannot reach or deteriorate. He is at the origin of time and is greater than time, ceaselessly renewing it. If to know God is eternal life, it is precisely because he is the Living One, the ever-new upsurge of life. Our Father is young. Not as we are young, unformed and amorphous, but with the unwavering, sovereign youth for which we yearn. He gives life, and his son is eternally born anew. To know him is, for us too, to be born of him in time. "Whoever believe that Jesus is the Christ has been begotten by God.... God has given us eternal life and this life is in his Son" (1 Jn 5:1; 5:11).

In other words, our experience of the Father is included in our experience of the resurrection. This may be one more reason why we understand so little about him. To the extent to which we take the gospel to be a moral code and Jesus a model of the past, we are living in ignorance of our own resurrection. If we are not born anew at every instant in the youth of the Lord, how can we be open to the intimate presence of our Father? Our living faith enables us to welcome the risen Christ and in him to become "children of God" (Jn 1:12). We are born of the Father by the coming of the Spirit into our lives. In the same thrust that frees us from slavery, the Spirit brings us to birth in the freedom of divine adoption (Gal 4:5 f; Rom 8:14-17).

Since we are one with Christ, we become sons and heirs with him (Gal 3:26-29). The twofold object of the promise is accomplished on the most personal level: the posterity is the incarnate son of God in whom we become children of God and the land we inherit is God's own life. Our experience of the fatherhood of God fulfills our deepest psychological aspirations. The security of a child is determined by the firmness and the tenderness his father shows him. Any failure in this domain can seriously impair his balance when he is an adult. Much of the anxiety that torments people in their forties stems from this. But we have no right to draw the conclusion that a filial feeling toward God is nothing more than a compensation for a human deficiency—even if this is so for many people. By no means. It is not a product of natural needs, nor is it a sublimation which simply substitutes God

for our human father. To be a child of God is the free gift of
the Spirit of God whom we can receive only at the highest
summit of our spirit. But this free gift is in accordance with
the deepest needs of our nature. Here, as everywhere else,
we discover the essential law of our being by which gratuitousness is necessary to us because it is free. A Christian
becomes adult when, going beyond the experience of fatherhood imposed on him by life, he opens himself to the discovery of the Father of whom he is freely born and whose perfection he can freely choose as his model. "You must
therefore be perfect just as your heavenly Father is perfect"
(Mt 5:48). Our relation with the Father can only reach its full
flowering in a heart that is purified and liberated, in a heart
that no longer sees him as an object or a means but which
loves him for himself, passionately and freely.

Here we see the other pole of our experience of the
Father. Not only do we come from him, but we tend toward
him: "The proof that you are sons is that God has sent the
Spirit of his Sons into our hearts: the Spirit that cries, 'Abba,
Father'" (Gal 4:6; Rom 8:16). Our striving for self-realization
reaches its goal within the thrust of the Spirit. In him the
whole of our being is turned toward the Father. "God is spirit,
and those who worship must worship in spirit and truth" (Jn
4:24). People sometimes talk about perfect charity as though
it were unattainable by ordinary human beings. And yet in
our better moments we are all capable of making other people happy for no other reason than that we want their happiness and we know that this free expression of love is the best
guarantee of our own joy. Why should we be unable to behave
in this way toward the Father? Through the Spirit who lives

in us and who is the love by which we live, we are capable of seeking God's joy for no other reason than himself and his joy. In the measure in which the Spirit is our rule of life, we are spontaneously capable of acting gratuitously. And the joy that we give our Father is the guarantee of our own joy, and no one can take it away from us (Jn 16:22). "It is to the glory of my Father that you should bear much fruit" (Jn 15:8). The fruit of our maturity bears within itself God's joy: to seek his joy gives our life its eternal flavor.

Everything comes from gratuitousness and must flower in gratuitousness. Love burgeons in us and reaches its full stature in a free communion with him who is the fullness of love. But do we feel we know the God we live with? Perhaps he is not yet a living person for some of us? And even if we are open to a personal communion with him, it may be that we have reduced him to a single person. This would be a form of theism, or natural religion, or the kind of Unitarian mysticism found in Islam. If God is one person, we are the most unfortunate of men, living with an idea, excluded from the flow of history and with no spiritual bonds with other men. Obviously God must be a personal God; otherwise each one of us, rich with the mystery of our own personal being, would be more than God. But he cannot be personal in the human way without being simply an alienating projection of ourselves. Corroboration of this is to be seen in the fact that no mono-personal religion has ever succeeded in saving man in the depths of his personality as well as in his social reality as a member of a human community located in time and space. If God is personal, it cannot be as, in our manner, a single nucleus open to communion with other persons. This would mean that either he is essentially indigent or, what would be worse, that he is an egoistical solitude. We can only reason thus far. But Jesus Christ both carries the demands of reason farther and responds to them: God is not only personal, he is the fullness of personal being, the communion of three Persons in perfect oneness. He is not composite, he is pure light (1 Jn 1-2). Communion between human persons can reach only a certain degree of unity, never perfect oneness. In God this oneness of light is possible because he is love (1 Jn 3-4), and each person is wholly "toward" the other.

The capacity to be turned "toward" another is the most divine attribute in man, but we shall reach maturity only when the divine flow of life has completely possessed us. This is what Paul speaks of as "the love of God (which) has been poured into our hearts by the Holy Spirit which has been given us" (Rom 5:5). God is love because he is Father, Son and Holy Spirit (1 Jn 4:7). So many Christians do not know that they are saying this when they profess faith in one God in three Persons. Often they only see an insoluble riddle in the formula. And many "spiritual" authors encourage this attitude by giving the impression that only a few "mystics" can actually have any experience of the Trinity. And yet God is love because he is the communion of three Persons in unity. All who are baptized live in this love, and to grow in the new life of baptism is to be more and more open to intimacy with God. Jesus is the event of the revelation of the Father to men, and this revelation is not reserved for a few wise or well-instructed persons able to maintain a privileged position. On the contrary, the mystery of the kingdom is hidden to the wise: "I bless you, Father, Lord of heaven and of earth, for hiding these things from the learned and the clever and revealing them to mere children" (Lk 10:21). The Father gives himself to the heart that is poor and gentle and patient, to the man who hungers for him who is merciful toward all, who lives in light and peace. The joy of the kingdom and God's true repose—goal of the epic of creation (Heb 3:7-4:11)—is accessible only to those whose hearts abide in the Spirit.

We are always in urgent need of conversion, but we must realize that, just as for the prodigal son, conversion is both a departure and return toward the Father, "So he left the place and went back to his father" (Lk 15:20). The mystery of God is not a metaphysical conundrum but the impact in our daily life of the gift of his son and of his Spirit. It is through this gift that he becomes the pivot and central event of every moment of our lives. To praise his name; to seek to do his will; to hasten the coming of the kingdom: to hunger each day for the true bread…all these phrases mean one and the same thing and can all be summed up in the fundamental impetus of our being expressed in the first word of our prayer: Father! Jesus' prayer becomes ours in the pleas of the Spirit who dwells in our hearts (Lk 11:2; Rom 8:15-16; 8:26-27).

If we live habitually turned toward the Father truly seeking his joy, we can live in a constant climate of joy, and the initial gift of grace matures into a response of thanksgiving. This is no doubt the reason why all the texts of the New Testament that refer to the Father breathe a special atmosphere of praise and thanksgiving. "Filled with joy by the Holy Spirit, he said, 'I bless you, Father'" (Lk 10:21). "Jesus said,

Father, I thank you for hearing my prayer" (Jn 11:41). "Father, the hour has come: glorify your Son so that your Son may glorify you" (Jn 17:1). "Blessed be God the Father" (Eph 1:3). Later Christian tradition expressed this mystery of joy in the saying that all true theology is doxology. Theology is the study of God, but God is not an object to be studied, he is someone to be recognized by the heart. The more one knows of him, the more one is lost in admiration before him. He can only be known by one who loves him, and the more one loves him the more one finds him admirable. Doxology is a thanksgiving to God, a reflection of the light flowing from him. To know God is to give him thanks. Our Father is a name that our heart murmurs in a song: "With gratitude in your hearts sing psalms and hymns and inspired songs to God; and never say or do anything except in the name of the Lord Jesus, giving thanks to God the Father through him" (Col 3:16-17).

CHAPTER SEVEN

The Kingdom, the Full Flowering of Love

The mystery of the covenant reveals God's true countenance. He is love, the fullness of personal communion, and the reciprocal relationship he establishes with us transforms us into his countenance. In Christ, God's countenance takes on a human likeness and our human experience becomes divine and reaches perfection in a filial turning toward the Father. This movement fills us with joy and makes us capable of loving. The event of the kingdom reveals just how far this development can take us. If God's beauty shines forth in man, then man must show in his way of living that God is communion in joy. And it is true that when we enter fully into the mode of being required by the covenant, our human relations are modified. The maturity that we glimpsed as the term of our exodus is expressed by the ease with which we face up to reality and develop harmonious relationships with others.

But let us take a look at the "mode of being" in the covenant to which we are called. From our earliest youth we are formed by others, either by reaction or by imitation. But we also reveal ourselves all the time in the kind of relations we establish with others. Someone has said that the quickest way to self is through others, and we have all witnessed the dangers of social isolation for a growing child or the deficiencies in someone who is entirely self-taught. In the religious life, any aspirations toward the life of a hermit should first be tested in a community. When a young monk is really capable of solitude, it is not from any lack of sociability but because he aspires to live his communion with the Mystical Body of Christ on a level of personal mystery. Whether we like it or not, other people are our necessary complement and we can measure our maturity by the degree of our responsibility toward them. We are born of and we grow through and for others.

Here again we see the pattern of the given elements of our social self and the original gratuitousness that they conceal. The poem of creation is the poem of our personality. We are made in the likeness of God, which means that we are "made toward" others. The poem becomes a love story because the "other" is the most beautiful gift that creation can offer. But the drama is that we refuse this and turn in upon ourselves in possessiveness. The bondage within us urges us to use others for our own interests, whereas our liberation would be to serve them for themselves. And so the success of our interpersonal relations demands that we experience a pasch. We have to make the transition from individualistic egoism to self-offering; we have to transform our impersonal collectivities into human communities; we have to establish a solidarity with others based on freedom in the place of an interdependence necessary for survival.

The human community prefigured by the kingdom of the Old Testament will only become a reality in the Spirit of the risen Christ. It is not given to us from the beginning. We have to build it. The gratuitousness inherent in our social relations is very far from being fully developed. Perhaps this is the reason why the Bible, when it is talking of the kingdom, uses images drawn from plant life, or building, from the body or from family life: it is a way of expressing the fact that the human community is something that must grow and develop organically and harmoniously. It is true that the kingdom is present, as a seed, in Christ, but the harvest—and, to a certain extent, even the preparation of the soil—still lies in the future. And so the kingdom is still the object of hope (Mt 6:10), and charity, which should be the supreme spontaneity of the Spirit within us, still has to be formulated as a commandment (Mt 5:43-48). It is not natural to us to love everyone as Christ loves (Jn 13:34-35).

THE FIRST DRAFT OF THE KINGDOM

It might seem that the first groping steps toward the kingdom in the old "disposition" are without interest for us, since in fact others can only become close to us when our hearts of stone have been transformed by the Holy Spirit into hearts of flesh (Ez 36:26). And yet the first rough sketches of charity do concern us, for Christ came not to abolish but to accomplish, and the building of his body rests on the foundations laid by the People of God before his coming.

From Moses to the deportation the story of the kingdom is the story of a people taking possession of a land and slowly finding its own cohesion. The particular sign that distinguishes this story from that of other peoples, in the overall political and social history of the times, is that it is both the story of God and the story of Israel. The political entity that begins to take shape is not simply the result of the socio-economic factors at work, it could only have been brought about within the context of the covenant. One could say that the theology underlying the books of the kingdom is a theology of fidelity to the covenant of Sinai (Dt 28-29). We shall now try to discern the central message of this theology in order to bring some light to bear on the preliminary conditions of true evangelical charity that are still valid.

The first element that strikes us is that Israel, as a people, is born of a liberation. The going out from Egypt made a nation out of a heterogeneous collection of tribes. This fact is important and can be seen to be true in modern times also: the demands of national unity are acknowledged once political independence is won. No one is astonished that it takes a long time to achieve effective unity, but first of all a people has to emerge from foreign domination. In the kingdom of God, the kingdom of love, this law of life holds good. We cannot live in harmony with others if we are not free. This is another case in which a sense of humor can be extremely useful, for when we uncover the real reasons for our disagreements with others, we have to admit that they usually come from ourselves. If, seeing this, we accept the effort of humility and hope that the pasch has shown to be so fruitful, we can free ourselves and reestablish a harmonious relationship with others. We shall never be too conscious of the fact that the movement that establishes a communion between ourselves and our fellows stems from an inner movement of self-liberation. Divine charity can only flourish in hearts that are free. This is one message that Exodus teaches about the mystery of the kingdom.

The Book of Deuteronomy (which means "the second law" and which insists that the law should reside in our hearts), in spite of the fact that the final version was probably written several centuries after the original, draws attention to another preliminary condition: the People of God is a chosen people. Obviously this has no racist or narrowly nationalistic meaning. It simply means that we are freely loved, that God does not owe us anything: "If Yahweh set his heart on you and chose you, it was not because you outnumbered other peoples: you were the least of all peoples. It was for love of you" (Dt 7:7-8). "Take yourselves for instance, brothers, at the time when you were called . . . those whom the world thinks common and contemptible are the ones that God has chosen" (1 Cor 1:26-31). The only reason for this choice is the gratuitousness of love: we are lovable only in that we are loved. But it is this very reason that allows us to love in turn. The result of our election is that we become "consecrated" beings freed from egoism and living by the Holy Spirit. "For you are a people consecrated to Yahweh your God; it is you that Yahweh our God has chosen to be his very own people" (Dt 7:6). "He has taken us out of the power of darkness and created a place for us in the kingdom of the Son he loves" (Col 1:13). Israel is the type and image of mankind. God has chosen every man and seeks to lead all men into the light of love. If we become aware of the love he bestows on us, then it is possible for us to love with the same gratuitousness. It is a characteristic of love that it can see every human being as lovable simply because he has been loved by God. In this way men come together at the very source of their being, bathed in the same grace. No deep community among men can be true or lasting if it is not bonded on this level. "We are to love, then, because he loved us first" (1 Jn 4:19); this is the consequence and fruit of God's election. "We have passed out of death and into life, and of this we can be sure because we love our brothers" (1 Jn 3:14). To love our fellows is the sign of our paschal consecration. To love someone is to know him in truth, to be born with him into the life of love (1 Jn 4:8; 5:1).

The Book of Joshua tells of the vicissitudes of the people settling down in the Promised Land. The Kingdom of Israel is established only after a victorious struggle. And for us, too, the kingdom of love can only be established with a struggle. The suffering endured while crossing the desert already indicates this: our struggle is not in opposition to others or in an attempt to dominate them; it is the struggle to conquer self in order to establish the inner unity necessary for peaceful communion with others. But the message contained in the story of the conquest of Canaan goes farther. Their common struggle united the clans of the house of Jacob, and for the first time they really experienced unity and solidarity, in spite of movements in which they reverted to tribalism (Jos 7:22). In our own conquest of the kingdom (Mt 11:12) we must also experience this liberating suffering. As we have seen, our liberation lies along the axis of our radical poverty. We must add that it is strengthened by our own labors. We have to sweat and strain with our fellow men in order to forge a deep fellowship. Just as God has not loved us from afar but by bearing the whole burden of our human condition including death, so our tender love for others must be lived close to them and by bearing their burdens. The wonder of it is that this is how we free ourselves: 'You should carry each other's troubles and fulfill the law of Christ," to love (Gal 6:2). And Christ, who took the weight of our sins in his own body on the cross so that we should become dead to our sins and live for holiness (1 Pt 2:24), reassures us: "My yoke is easy and my burden light" (Mt 11:30). "Our love is not to be just words or mere talk, but something real and active" (1 Jn 3:18), for God's Kingdom "is not just words, it is power" (1 Cor 4:20) and "there is nothing I cannot master with the help of the One who gives me strength" (Phil 4:13).

In this respect the Book of Judges is reassuringly realistic. It follows the fluctuations of an emerging nation showing how, when the people are unfaithful to the covenant, they fall back into bondage and are divided amongst themselves and, when they turn back to Yahweh, they free themselves once again and are restored to national unity. This is the rhythm of charity. When it is lived "in deeds and in truth," it reveals the indissoluble bond that binds each man to God and to his fellows. As soon as we abandon the one we lose the other. And since we are in communion with another at the highest point of our spiritual freedom, it is understandable that we have to live on that level if we are to remain open to others. Another can only be close to us in the closeness of a personal love. Apart from that, we can be moved by altruistic feelings to spend ourselves in philanthropic activities, but we cannot go very far along this road. We all throw up so many barriers to others that the movement of communion is slowed and finally comes to a halt. "Anyone who says, 'I love God,' and hates his brother, is a liar" (1 Jn 4:20). And, on the other hand, "we can be sure that we love God's children if we love God himself" (1 Jn 5:2). It is the same movement that bears us toward him and toward our brothers, and it flows from the same demands within us not of activism but of spiritual freedom which recognizes our inherent poverty and opens us in a gesture of welcome to the mystery of another being.

Several things can be learned about the kingdom in the flavorful variety of stories contained in the two Books of Samuel. But one in particular is very important at this stage of development of God's people: the significance of a king. It is obvious that the authors have a distinct preference for David, a king according to God's heart. And David is in fact an authentic incarnation of the notion of authority amongst God's People. It is Yahweh who is the one and only King and Shepherd of his people. Israel adopts a monarchic form of government, but the role of the highest authority is to guarantee the people's fidelity to the covenant. He cannot use his position of honor to lord it over the people. "You know that among the pagans the rulers lord it over them, and their great men make their authority felt. This is not to happen amongst you" (Mt 20:25-26). The position of royalty is subject to exactly the same ambivalence that exists in all our relations to others: domination and service. The original temptation is, once again, apparent. Authority is necessary to safeguard the common good, otherwise love is impossible. But the healthy roots of authority are always in danger of being contaminated by the perversity of possessive egoism and authority turns to using others instead of serving them. The greater a man's responsibility the more he needs to be spiritually free. All of us have some measure of authority, and it inevitably degenerates as soon as we use it, even unknowingly, to express our own interest, our own need to dominate, our own incurable vanity. Authority which only exists in relation to charity demands dispossession of self and self-giving. "The greatest among you must behave as if he were the youngest, the leader as if he were the one who serves" (Lk 22:26-27). Only in his manner can authority be a redemption, a liberation and a source of happiness for all: "The Son of Man came not to be served but to serve, and to give his life as a ransom for many" (Mt 20:28).

We see the illustration of this in the two Books of Kings which recount the drama of the royal institution as it evolved into a paganized, political domination. When they ceased to serve God, the kings of Israel ceased to serve their own people. The people, being unfaithful to God, were unfaithful to love. The inevitable result was a return to slavery and the scattering of the nation. This is the culminating point of the disastrous period of the Judges. The cohesiveness of the kingdom, therefore, is in direct ratio to the people's fidelity to God-Love. By the very fact of its disintegration, the short-lived kingdom of Israel shows up the indestructible newness of the true kingdom in which all men are brothers, that true kingdom which is God himself.

LOVE IS OUR KINGDOM

"From that moment Jesus began his preaching with the message, 'Repent, for the kingdom of heaven is close at hand'" (Mt 4:17). "The time has come; he said 'and the kingdom of God is close at hand. Repent, and believe the Good News'" (Mk 1:15). It is good news indeed to learn that all men, however antagonistic they may be, can become close to each other. This is the absolute criterion against which we can always check whether we are truly living men or not and whether the God we live with is the true, living God. All our ideologies and all our principles are nothing but a hoax and an alienation if they fall short of this total truth.

The old order, although it offered some tentative indications of the universal kingdom, was radically powerless to achieve it. The law, although fundamentally healthy, could do no more than assure an exterior, social cohesion. Only the coming of the Spirit could rectify and liberate us from within and bring us together without barriers. The kingdom of Heaven is near at hand and always new because God is near at hand, having taken flesh in our human condition. The coming of the living One makes everything into life, the coming of him who is free, frees us, the coming of love in person into the world restores the world to the communion of persons.

The mode of human relations is changed and made radically new. Our unity no longer lies in principles or in activity but in someone, and the law which guides us is no longer contained in a code, it is a personal presence dwelling in our hearts. Finally, we are no longer a mass of isolated individuals or subjects to an exterior power of authority, we are a "line of kings, priests to serve" (Rv 1:6). This is the most distinctive characteristic that unites all men in Christ: we are a priestly people. And yet the priesthood of all Christians is almost unknown to most people who think of it as a piece of pious rhetoric of Catholic Action theorists or as a hangover from Reformation Protestantism. The sociological structure of the Church is so much more visible. And yet, although the social structures of the Church are necessary to the kingdom of love, as we shall see later, they are subservient to love. The question here is the fundamental nature of the belonging which makes each one of us an ecclesial being. For this new communion given to men by the Spirit of the risen Christ is the Church. It is the eternal mystery of the Church present in germ in the first man and brought to fulfillment and spread abroad by Christ.

Love is our kingdom. This is not the love of an ill-defined philanthropy but the divine holiness given to man by Christ and made manifest "through the Church" in the Spirit (Eph 3:10). Even the first covenant was open to this reality: "I will count you a kingdom of priests, a consecrated nation" (Ex 19:6), and this is a kingdom that Christ came to accomplish. "You are a chosen race, a royal priesthood, a consecrated nation, a people set apart to sing the praises of God who called you out of the darkness into this wonderful light. Once you were not a people at all and now you are the people of God" (1 Pt 2:9-10). Our fundamental priesthood, therefore, is that we are risen with Christ, that we have passed from darkness to the light of holiness. To be holy as our heavenly Father is holy (Mt 5:48) is to be of transparent simplicity with no more dissension between what we are and what we appear to be, between what we are and what we do. When Paul writes to his Christians—who were certainly not much better than we are—he quite simply calls them "saints," for they are saints by their new nature and by their calling. "To the church of God in Corinth, to the holy people of Jesus Christ, who are called to take their place among all the saints everywhere" (1 Cor 1:1-2). "Thanking the Father who has made it possible for you to join the saints and with them to inherit the light" (Col 1:12). This sanctity stands in contrast to "the present wicked world" (Gal 1:4) as light contrasts with darkness and love with egoism. When love is our life, we are living the sanctity of our baptismal priesthood and we are able to do so because we are a new creation in Christ (2 Cor 5:17). We are a kingdom of priests because the new life of the risen Christ has been communicated to us through baptism.

If we are to understand that charity is not a moral value, however perfect, we must appreciate the reality of this priesthood. Charity is a total experience. It is the Church. Why does the Bible use the notion of priesthood to express the essential holiness of love? It is, no doubt, because the priesthood conferred on us by baptism is the consecration of the whole person and his whole life to "sing the praises of God" who is love and liberty (1 Pt 2:9). We have already noted that the goal of the first Exodus was to go and adore God (Ex 3:12). But since the fountainhead of charity is the goal of our inner, paschal journey to the kingdom, and since to love is to offer continual adoration, we can see that the kingdom of love is a communion in light and adoration, in other words, a holy and priestly communion. Later we shall discuss the eternal liturgy, but we can say here that it is lived already on earth in every slightest movement of true love which passes from our

176

hearts into effective action. And we can see that just as Israel's basic infidelity lay in living as a political nation rather than as a priestly people according to their true vocation, this is also our basic infidelity, both personally and communally, in the Church.

If this is the manner of our belonging to the kingdom, then to say that a baptized Christian is risen from the dead or that he has consecrated his life to love are two ways of saying the same thing. From this we can draw some practical conclusions. It is false to say that we can love someone "in Christ" if we don't really love him personally. It would amount to saying that we cover over a humanity that is repugnant to us with the "veil" of Christ. But to love is to make holy, to consecrate all that is contained in the human by freeing it from sin. Sin is the only repugnance possible to a heart that lives in the Spirit. Charity effects what the love of oneself—which is even more difficult—should effect in us: liberation from the captivity of sin and egoism into the realm of life. There is no such thing as the "spiritual" without the incarnation. The Holy Spirit is the spirit of Christ of whose body we are all members in fact or by vocation. As in Ezekiel's vision, the Spirit is the breath of God restoring cohesion and life to the dried bones that we are. We know very well how lifeless and dried up we can be in regard to others. Our God is far more human than we are: "My heart recoils from it, my whole being trembles at the thought. . . . For I am God, not man: I am the Holy One in your midst and have no wish to destroy" (Hos 11:8-9). And it is worse to destroy someone's reputation than to take his life. St. John compares a lack of love to a murder: "To hate your brother is to be a murderer"

(1 Jn 3:15): most of the time we need seek no farther to uncover the cause of our spiritual sterility. The death-wish which poisons all our human relations is banished from our new being risen from the dead. Our daily resurrection consists in loving. Love is life, eternal life, the tireless power of life. Only a truly human love can work miracles. "What I want is love, not sacrifice" (Hos 6:6). When we love we are the priests of the universe and communicate true life to our fellowmen.

This is the priestly power of the transfiguration of the universe that Jesus entrusted to us when he gave us the "new Commandment." "I give you a new commandment: love one another" (Jn 13:34). It is amazing and even scandalous that Christian catechism still retain the formula: to love one's neighbor as oneself. Of course it is not false. The phrase comes from the Old Law, and Paul uses it more than once (Rom 13:9; Gal 5:14). It is extremely demanding, for it goes further than the requirements of justice—the first manifestation of charity (Mt 7:12)—and is really part of the new covenant, for to love oneself requires the peace of soul of one who is already set free in the new life. But Christ's New Commandment goes much further. Left to ourselves we love others simply because and insofar as they appear lovable to us. But Jesus does not love us just because we are lovable. He loves us to make us lovable. We are lovable because he loves us. Whereas we admire things because they are beautiful, he looks at them and in so doing makes them beautiful. God's gaze bestows beauty on all things, and his love gives them their goodness; this is why, when we really know someone in depth, he is always a source of wonderment and admiration.

This is the way we should know and love other beings. Not that we are, of ourselves, sources of beauty and goodness, but in the risen Christ God's light and his love have really been given to us as ours. Moreover, it is a characteristic of the love of friendship to re-create one's friend each time he disappoints one. God re-creates us unceasingly, in spite of our disappointing lack of fidelity. And so "we are to love, then, because he loved us first" (1 Jn 4:19), and to "forgive each other as soon as a quarrel begins. The Lord has forgiven you; now you must do the same" (Col 3:13). "And forgive us our debts, as we have forgiven those who are in debt to us" (Mt 6:12). "It can only be to God's glory, then, for you to treat each other in the same friendly way as Christ treated you" (Rom 15:7). It is clearly not a question of imitating Christ from afar or of following a juridical pattern. It is the same inner movement that in him both receives and transmits the same divine light and love. It is "God, all things to all men," and it is the kingdom.

One would have to read the whole Gospel over and over to see how charity is the cement of unity. This is what we have to live. Nothing else. Everything comes together in one in the kingdom of love, and all that Our Lord says and does is only the varied expression of the one divine charity that penetrates the whole of man and through him the whole of creation. It is this love that is the pearl for which we must sell all we have (Mt 13:14 f). It can be perceived only by the "little flock," the humble of heart, for it is not present in prestigious deeds and resounding phrases (Lk 12:32). This is the love that is proclaimed by the word of God and received in faith (Mt 13). Its growth takes place in secret and it brings forth fruits in patience (Mt 13). It is given freely: Workers are hired at any hour of the day in the kingdom of love, and the joy that is received is greater than any wages (Mt 20:1-16). It is lived by the poor in spirit (Mt 5:3), and its greatness is to be "as little children" (Mt 18:1-4). It must be sought for actively, for it is not natural to the heart of man; but when a man finds it, he finds too that all things are given with it, all things become possible (Mt 6:33). This love is the authentic fulfillment of the will of the Father for whom to will is the same as to love (Mt 7:21). Christ identifies himself with all men in this love (Mt 23:34 f) which demands a constant conversion: to love is to be reborn (Mt 18:3; Jn 3:3 f). It is a love that shows its tenderness in watching and waiting (Mt 25:1-13). It is the ultimate object of our prayer, "Thy Kingdom come," that will be won not by renouncing all our own efforts but by joining our efforts to our prayer in a total commitment to the coming of the kingdom (Mt 6:10). The miracles that Jesus works are a living manifestation of this love, for love works the miracle of restoring life where only sorrow, discouragement and death held sway. Love is stronger than death or any kingdom built on force (Dn 2-7; Wis 4 f; Sg 8:6). Love is a sign that God is present, and with him living man (Mt 12:28). Finally, this is the love to which the Church, "communion in love," must bear witness. (Mt 10:7; Acts 8:12; 14:21; 19:8). "By this love you have for one another, everyone will know that you are my disciples" (Jn 13:35).

The miracle of love may seem wonderful to us when we contemplate it in the Gospels, but we always tend to be unrealistic when we read Scripture, we also need to feel its implications for ourselves. One of its most fundamental implications concerns the truth of our relations with others. We are so heavily handicapped by our hangovers from childhood or later experience that we rarely perceive others as they really are. Our subjectivism erects a wall between them and us, and very often when we believe we are giving welcome to another we have simply met a projection of ourselves. The need for truth implies here too an unyielding liberation. Just consider the mechanism that sets off our antipathy; why do certain things that people do irritate us while others leave us indifferent? Objectively they can be equally reprehensible or equally commendable; this is not the criterion of our spontaneous reaction. Very often we are irritated when we see another person behaving in a way that our ideal self has rejected and condemned, rightly or wrongly, for ourselves. In fact, as any psychologist can tell us, we are still capable of this "forbidden" behavior, and it is our own reflection in the other person that triggers our antipathy. A pacifying liberation can only be attained by the pasch described earlier: by the attitude of the Publican who returned home after his prayer in the Temple "justified." The same kind of mechanism operates in spontaneous sympathies. We like agreeable company, and often we nurture a high regard for someone who is intelligent because he shares our own opinions or for another because he shares our sentiments about things. We should beware of simply admiring ourselves in others. We are tangled up in ourselves to an unbelievable extent, and we can never be too aware of this. And here too we need a sense of humor to ferret out our false pretences and recapture the simplicity of heart without which others will always remain closed to us and will never become our "neighbors."

Another realistic demand of the gospel, which stems from our royal priesthood, is that love must take the initiative gratuitously if we are to be freed from the prison of ourselves. Charity is nurtured by signs, and an egoistic attitude demands signs of love as a due, whereas a priestly attitude of self-offering gives signs of love rather than demanding them. But this supposes that we have faith in others. Signs or tokens are not enough. The promise is a mystery of faith and of signs because the object of the promise—a land and a posterity—is brought to fulfillment in the kingdom. Over and above everything else and to "keep them together and complete them," we must "put on love" (Col 3:14).

It is charity that edifies—in the laborious, work-a-day sense that the authentic Christian tradition attributes to this word (1 Cor 8:1). It builds a new city for God and men (Rv 21). It builds a new body, the body of the risen Christ in which we, the dead members, are restored to life (Eph 4). The whole of Christian experience can be summed up in this one word: love. And when we say that our Christian condition is priestly, it is a way of expressing the meaning of sacramental life in the kingdom of love, for the body of Christ grows mysteriously through the sacramental life. But the sacraments are only signs, however effective, that must have their prolongation in our daily life. This is the sacramental sense of the service of others. It is a sacrament of God, for Christ identified himself with the lowliest of men. And the act of giving that takes us out of ourselves to a communion with him is also sacramental: it is the eternal liturgy of love, the loving attitude of self-offering in which our whole personality reaches fulfillment.

This supposes that the life of the Spirit is vigorous within us, readying us constantly for the sacrifices of obligation. This word sacrifice is one of the words that an impoverished piety has most successfully emptied of all meaning. But if we put it back into the vivifying context of the priestly kingdom formed by the people of God, it recaptures its full significance of resurrection. The sacrifice is that which makes something sacred, holy, in other words, which places it in the light of love. If love is to be the mainspring of our activity, its fire must burn brightly within us. This is the meaning of the prayer of the heart. As some of the Church Fathers expressed it: the heart is the altar and we are the offering. For ultimately God and other human beings do not want us to give things but to give ourselves. Our presence can become a spiritual "clearing" in which others can breathe freely and be themselves. And the joy we seek after so avidly will no longer be something we grasp for ourselves but the fruit of our own self-giving.

PART THREE

THE ENCOUNTER WITH DEATH

He who knows the mystery of the Cross and of the Tomb knows the reason for the existence of all creatures.

—Maximus the Confessor

CHAPTER EIGHT

Exile, or the Proving of Love

The Bible has revealed so much about our integral human experience that we may feel that it can have no more to teach us. Since we now realize that our experience of Christ reaches its fullness in love, and since love is the final coming of the kingdom in our human lives, all we have to do is live by that love and all will be accomplished. But we still need to delve deeper into our own experience, for if we really want to integrate all the elements of our daily life in Christ, we must still see that there are in fact many negative spots in our existence that need to be looked at more closely. In theory we know that our pasch progresses from the seeds of creation to the fruit of the kingdom, but we also know that all too often the only fruits we seem to gather are failure, sin and death. Our love is not so perfect that it needs no purification; our freedom is not so great that it can never be endangered. A new stage in the history of God's people teaches us something in this respect: it is the period of exile, or deportation.

187

For us it is the equivalent of a time in which our love is put to the test, in which the kingdom is called into question. It is a time of purification of the very roots of our freedom.

The first experience of a kingdom ends in disaster for Israel. The Babylonian invasion of 587 B.C. put an end to the dynasty of David, scattered Abraham's descendants, destroyed the capital and the temple and finally carried off the people into captivity far from their Promised Land. All their cherished dreams seem to crumble when they are exiled, the promise to Abraham seems to be lost beyond all hope, and everything is called into question as though history had stepped backward a thousand years in time. After many years of hard work we find ourselves faced with the same disastrous reckoning, whether it be on the level of our personal lives or in our social or ecclesial commitments. We still seem to be struggling with the same inner divisions as before; our family and social life has not been as rewarding as we had expected, and growth of the kingdom in the world after two thousand years seems to be a spectacular failure. What is the point of all the efforts and generosity that have been expanded? We don't have to have reached old age to be tempted by the disillusioned "wisdom" of Qoheleth: "This too is vanity and chasing of the wind" (Qo 2:26). Much of modern philosophy, fascinated by the absurd and by nothingness, echoes this deep disillusionment with life, and one is led to wonder whether, in spite of gigantic technical advances, man is any more human than in the past. At some point most of us have to face up to the question of disillusionment when we realize our limitations—and the higher our early ideals the greater the risk of falling into bitter cynicism. By contrast with the kingdom that we are seeking to establish at the peak of man's freedom, we cannot help but be crushed by the evidence that points to the new bonds of servitude we are constantly forging for ourselves. What is the use of it all? And we come around, full cycle, to the first question: "to be or not to be": "There is only one serious philosophical problem—suicide" (Camus).

It is precisely at this point that the substance and fullness of the Christian experience strike us. If failure, whether of our own making or not, were not in some way integrated into our total picture of life, at least half of what constitutes our life would be irrevocably absurd, contaminating with absurdity our whole existence. All the false solutions that man has elaborated by himself throughout the centuries are utopian. No philosophical or religious system in which suffering, sin, death and the flow of history are neglected or passed over in silence can satisfy our basic need, however bright a light it may shed on many aspects of life. The reason why any such system—whether it be Islam, Marxism or liberal materialism—gains so many adherents is simply that social pressures and spiritual "under-development" combine to blind man to the full scope of his personal drama. But some of the essential elements are nevertheless missing, and no compensatory substitutions can overcome the resulting imbalance. Even the philosophies of despair, whether their emphasis is on the will to power or on disengagement, are an admission of impotence, and the modern generation is beginning to discount them completely.

But in Christ everything is integrated. Failure, sin and death, which seem to be in radical contradiction to the flowering of life, are caught up in life. Christ accepted the whole of our human condition including the burden of sin, failure and death. If he were only a model on an ethical level we could not take him seriously. But he, the living one, went to the furthest frontiers of our condition in order to win it over to life. This is the dramatic meaning of the cross that is prefigured in the story of the deportation. In Christ everything has a meaning and there is no margin of waste in our lives, no event left hanging in the no-man's land of meaninglessness. The cross is the truth of the resurrection which restores life to every area of our experience. The power of death, at work on all levels of our personal and social being, is induced to produce fruits of life. Deep down in our experience of absurdity the ultimate meaning of our adventure reveals itself. The marks of death, forming a contrasting pattern in our lives with the marks of our pasch, are integrated into the overall pattern of light.

The cross marks the decisive turning point in our journey; it is the spiritual point of convergence of all our constituent parts. We can perhaps see this more clearly if we consider how it is illustrated in the Bible. The phases we have passed through so far run from the creation through the promise, the pasch, exodus and the covenant to the kingdom. And the downfall that the deportation represents seems to throw us back to the time before the promise. But this is only in appearance. In fact, it expresses reality at a deeper level. In exile, we become firmly grounded on the rock of our own painful experience. It is the same theme as that of the promise played in a minor key. And from here on our own ill-defined melody builds up toward a new pasch, a new exodus, a new covenant and an infinite liturgy heralding the final establishments of the kingdom.

The Babylonian Captivity is analogous to the period of bondage in Egypt. Historically, it is simply a repetition by an Eastern power of the pattern established by a Western power. But there is a significant theological difference. During the captivity in Egypt the People of God was still amorphous. In leaving Egypt it leaves the first slavery of its own chaotic non-identity, just as we, through baptism, are delivered from the bondage of original sin. But in the case of the Babylonian Captivity, Israel falls into bondage by its own fault just as we are enslaved by our own personal sin. This is why, immediately before and during the exile, Israel's responsibility for its own sin becomes clearer. The nation has to go through a totally new phase. When they come out from Egypt, and similarly when we are baptized, it is God who does practically everything. But to return from Babylon and, for us, to turn back from our own waywardness, a true conversion of the heart is necessary. And so the time of exile becomes the time in which everything must be personalized. In the literature of Israel this is illustrated by the artifice of showing sin in the form of a person: the Devil. The story of man and the origins of sin in the world through the intervention of Satan is written at this period (Gn 3). The Babylonian Captivity is the figure of the crucifixion and is seen as the counterattack against Satan which brings about the final victory of the word, the conquest of all darkness by light. Christ on the cross is man who descends to the depths of human chaos to establish the reign of peace. And as we are one with him in his death and resurrection, every instant of our lives can become an encounter with death emerging into victorious life.

Every stage of our spiritual journey reveals something more of God's true countenance, and at this point we suddenly come face to face with the most astounding aspect of his tender love: we see that he is vulnerable. The cross lays bare the most hidden wounds of our nature, but it also lays bare the human truth of God's wound. We usually think that sin and the mortal wounds it gouges out in our being are our misfortune alone. Whereas, in fact, God is so woven into our history and into our very flesh that our sin is God's misfortune even more deeply than it is our own. He is ours and we are his in an indestructible partnership. On the cross this mystery of oneness is exposed, not in any sublime realization of ourselves, but in the prosaic truth of our condition: our wounds are his. If we were one with him only in our flashes of liberty and gratuitous love it would not mean much, but we are one with him even in our shortcomings and in our despair. And it is this that frees us. We can never be alone again since we exist in Christ. His way of teaching us is wonderfully realistic: when he wants to reveal himself to us, he first of all makes us see our own sin. Our sin is diametrically opposed to love and to him, but within our sinful state he is closer to us than we are to our own divided selves.

It is perhaps this realistic simplicity which is most disconcerting to us. When we are discouraged we feel that he is so far away, whereas in fact it is we who are far away in exile, not from him but from ourselves. We only have to get back to our own truth in order to get back to him. There are no more waste products, no more dead zones in our lives.

Our suffering and even our infidelities are paths he walks with us—the paths of the cross. How does this lead to our resurrection?

LOVE SHOWS UP SIN

Love is the original and ultimate harmony of all that exists. Sin is only a discordant note within the total orchestration. The more our lives are attuned to the harmony of love, the keener our perception of every discordant note. We do not live in a monotonous repetition of notes. Personally and in community the melody of our life grows fuller and richer. As the kingdom nears fulfillment, the enemy comes out into the open more and more. But in Christ all humanity is drawn toward sovereign life, and death's counter-attacks turn into a new victory for life. In the history of mankind, as well as in the personal life story of each one of us, this combat with sin is the price we must pay for the coming of the kingdom. "Rebellion is at its work already, but in secret" (2 Thes 2:7). This is the counterpoint to the work of the kingdom. The coexistence of sin and love is the message contained in the parable of the tares and the wheat (Mt 13:24-43) as well as in the passages of the Gospel concerning the last days. "And with the increase of lawlessness, love in most men will grow cold; but the man who stands firm to the end will be saved" (Mt 24:12-13). Love is constantly in danger in our lives, but the trials we undergo are destined to "yield a harvest through perseverance" (Lk 8:5). If there were no trials and no perseverance, we could hardly call our liberation our own. But we, ourselves, are the harvest of our love.

193

We can understand this relatively easily with respect to the evils that befall us through no fault of our own. But can this still be valid where our own sin is concerned? What does sin mean in our lives? As long as we consider this only from the point of view of the law, we cannot understand it, for in this perspective it is simply disobedience, and the guilt it engenders simply another ailment within us, one more faulty contact in our own circuit. But if we look at it in the light of our spiritual freedom, we can see the full, dramatic reality and, at the same time, the possibility of the victory of love. Our deepest personal sin does not occur in relation to any moral principle but in relation to someone: God and our fellows, inseparably one. It kills love at its roots, for it simply forgets those toward whom our power of loving should be turned. "My people have committed a double crime: they have abandoned me, the fountain of living water, only to dig cisterns for themselves, leaky cisterns that hold no water" (Jer 2:13). We need to have experienced the wonderful gift of the Spirit, true spring of the water of eternal life, welling up within us (Jn 4:14) to be able to comprehend the depths of this forgetting that is sin.

"I reared sons, I brought them up, but they have rebelled against me. The ox knows its owner and the ass its master's crib, Israel knows nothing, my people understand nothing" (Is 1:2-3). "I pastured them, and they were satisfied; once satisfied, their hearts grew proud, and so they came to forget me" (Hos 13:6). In a heart replete with self how can there be room for one atom of love? Our sin, even more than a forgetting, is the insensitivity of spoilt children, and we slip toward death once we cease to hunger for love. And yet that hunger is so much a part of us that we always seek to satisfy it, and this is how our sin becomes a self-deluding: "I am going to court my lovers, she said, who give me my bread and water, my wool, my flax, my oil and my drink. She would not acknowledge, not she, that I was the one who was giving her the corn, the wine, the oil, and who freely gave her that silver and gold of which they have made Baals . . . she made offerings to the Baals and decked herself with rings and necklaces to court her lovers, forgetting me" (Hos 2:7-13). It should be impossible to read passages such as this from the Prophets and not be clear sighted about our own sin: forgetfulness, infidelity, ingratitude, rebelliousness, infantile-self-idolatry. The Prophets give us the background we need to understand the significance of Jesus' words about sin (Lk 5; 7:31-50; 8:9-10; 11:14-52; 13:15).

"Only acknowledge your guilt: how you have apostatized from Yahweh your God, how you have flirted with strangers and have not listened to my voice" (Jer 3:13). "And I was thinking how I wanted to rank you with my sons, and give you a country of delights, the fairest heritage of all the nations! I had thought you would call me: *My Father*, and would never cease to follow me. But like a woman betraying her lover, the house of Israel has betrayed me" (Jer 3:19-20). In this climate we should be incapable of judging our sin dispassionately as though we were noting a moral deficiency; it should strike us to the heart. Our sin is a revelation of the folly of God's love because it shows up the frivolity of our response.

Our personal sins are not like a volcanic island suddenly erupting out of a smooth sea. They are the craggy peaks of the long chain of mountains that constitute our native density gradually being eroded away by love. Just as in the growth of love in a marriage relationship every act of infidelity has meaning in the ongoing process of emotional purification of husband and wife, so it is the slow unfolding of our relationship with God. No two acts of infidelity are alike except in their purely moral and legal aspects. In the context of the unique, personal relationship that God forges with each one of us, an act of sin is far more than an impersonal trespass. It is the void in us that betrays our deep need for the One we have slighted, the dreadful absence of him who should be our inspiring presence. In other words, because we are risen from the dead, sin takes on an entirely different meaning. It is no longer the absurd experience of death that throws us back each time a little farther into our solitude. It becomes an emptiness that is hunger, hunger for life and for a presence. And our guilt opens a breach in us through which God can reach and stir our sluggish hearts.

Here we see the very clear difference between the ethical and the Christian meaning of sin. The psychological experience of sin is the experience of a great emptiness, of the vanity of a fleeting gain, of a certain disgust. This feeling reveals a truth which is not only on the psychological level. It shows that when we sin, we think we are in pursuit of true worth . . . only to find that we have gained nothing of worth. This is the essential absurdity of sin: it is absolutely meaningless. The Christian perception does not repudiate these notions, but it goes farther. It is true that man does not really love his own sin and gives himself up to it more by fascination than by choice, as though to an inevitable bondage (Jdt 3).

Outside the context of the covenant sin is the absurd experience of death within us. But in the context of the Christian life that is no longer wholly true. The absurdity has been shown up; death has already been illuminated by life. A Christian's sin exists in relation to a personal presence that never leaves him. The only sin by which man could possibly lay hold of death definitely would be absolute despair. But when a man reaches this point, is he completely responsible for his choice? Despair is really the suicide of someone who goes on living. But as long as a man continues to face up to existence, he has not despaired either of himself or of God, even if he continues to seek for absolutes in things which have only relative value. In the dynamic of Christian life, sin unrelentingly reveals love because it forces us to renew hope. And hope

> is not deceptive...but what proves that God loves us is that Christ died for us while we were still sinners. Having died to make us righteous, is it likely that he would now fail to save us from God's anger? When we were reconciled to God by the death of his Son, we were still enemies; now that we have been reconciled, surely we may count on being saved by the life of his Son. (Rom 5:5-10)

And so for us the tragedy of our sin takes place within the context of an earlier and indestructible reconciliation.

Henceforth, "those who are in Christ are not condemned" (Rom 8:1). Obviously this does not mean that we can no longer sin, but it does mean that sin can no longer do away with hope. Henceforth life is first; our sin cannot arrest it. Love is first; our infidelity cannot wear it down. Too many people are pulled up short by their sins as though they constituted a dead-end, whereas the Good News of Christ crucified is precisely that they can become paths leading to a new and greater love. Many Christians are paralyzed by their uneasy conscience because they live with a God who is a distant master. They do not yet know Christ, undying presence of the Father and "distributor of the Holy Spirit" (Gregory Nazianzen). These are the people who receive the sacrament of pardon in order to quiet their conscience instead of seeking reconciliation with the Father simply for his joy. A peaceful conscience is included in "all these other things" that are promised to those who seek, first of all, the kingdom (Mt 6:33).

We must not forget that the exile comes after the kingdom and the covenant. Without the covenant our personal sin is a tragedy that imprisons us within ourselves: in the context of the covenant it is a turning point opening us to a release of life. The formation of an adult conscience requires that we reverse our perspective in this way, for it is the only way by which we can envisage our sin as a sickness affecting our love instead of as an organic imbalance. In other words, if our conscience is barely formed, we judge our sins according to the dictates of our self-esteem, whereas a truly Christian conscience "renewed by a spiritual revolution" (Eph 4:23) judges it according to the sensitivity of true love. The many inevitable disagreements in the life of a married couple can always be dispelled in a deeper understanding if each partner, instead of feeling them as a personal guilt which wounds his pride, can see them as a hurt for the other. True reconciliation can never be founded on a desire to restore one's own good conscience. It is based on a movement toward the other simply because one loves him. Even in our consciousness of our own sin we have to make the transition from self-love to gratuitous love. Only in this humble consciousness can sin be seen in its true light not as total absurdity but as the lie of our own pride which sets up the idol of self for our adoration. Also, this open transparency to God is the only way of getting rid of the widespread error by which we consider the worst sins to be those of the flesh. When we discussed the body, we saw clearly that sin lies only in the heart. Only a sub-Christian conscience that puts sociobiological taboos in the place of a sense of God could so distort the scale of values. Sin is not the infringement of a prohibition, it is a slighting of love. "What shortcoming did your fathers find in me that led them to desert me? Vanity they pursued, vanity they became" (Jer 2:5).

THE CROSS IS GOD'S WOUND AS WELL AS MAN'S

When we sin, we wound both ourselves and God. The fact that the Bible never considers sin in itself, but always in the perspective of a dialogue with God and of a healing, is very significant. The covenant teaches us to avoid moralizing, but it also teaches us to avoid the simpleminded indifference of amoralism. The demands of the Spirit are exacting, but they are the only way to truth and freedom. The truth which sets us free is the truth of the cross (Jn 8:31-36; 18:37).

Jesus fulfills all the prophecies in his crucifixion. His insistence, throughout his teaching, that he has come to "fulfill" the law and the Prophets is not a formula of speech for the purpose of argument. The embryonic truth contained in the teaching of the Prophets is, in the most real sense, brought to perfection in the life, death and resurrection of Christ. The Prophets spoke: Jesus is the living word. They announced our liberation: Jesus sets us free. He fulfills the promise because he, personally, is the word; he *is* what he says. He is not only the word that is uttered, he is the word that is given (Is 55:10-11). As St. John likes to emphasize, his "hour" contains in one dense moment the whole drama of God and man that is played out in time. "Those days," evoked on almost every page of the Prophets, are lived in their fullness on the cross. This is "the Lord's Day," on which his whole plan reaches fulfillment. When Jesus cries out "It is accomplished" before giving up his Spirit, it is the decisive moment of judgment which saves or condemns (Jn 19:30; 12:27-32).

Our experience of the covenant teaches us that Christ's sufferings are not the price paid for our "ransom" in the ordinary sense of the word. It is true we have been ransomed. Numerous biblical texts use this image: Exodus 6:6-7; Isaiah 62:11-12; 63:9; Titus 2:13-14. "You have all been bought and paid for" (1 Cor 7:23). But we must understand this correctly. We belong to God (Ex 19:5-6). He does not have to pay ransom money to any one of us, least of all to the Devil, as though the Devil had acquired rights over us. Any word, when it is applied to God, must be understood in a special and unique way, and the word ransom—or redemption—is no exception. We are his, but when we sin we claim to belong only to ourselves, to exist only for ourselves. And this calls for a new way of "belonging" in which God reveals to what extent he is *ours* by giving himself completely to us.

"With God on our side who can be against us? Since God did not spare his own Son, but gave him up to benefit us all" (Rom 8:32). The cross is the revelation of the lengths to which the mystery of the covenant goes. God does not save us from afar. From the bottom of our absence from God Jesus cries out: "My God, my God, why have you deserted me?" (Mt 27:46). He actually lives what we live when we sin: the desolation of absolute solitude. To love means "to become" the beloved. Is it possible that God can "become us" to the point of being with us in our separation from himself? This is what we are affirming. This is the "ransom," the redemption: he is ours even at the farthermost point of our absence from him, so that even there we can find him and be his once again. When we say that someone is "dear" to us, we do not really mean it very often. Only God means it. We have cost him the full price of his self-giving: "Do not be afraid, for I have redeemed you; I have called you by your name, you are mine…because you are precious in my eyes…and I love you" (Is 43:1-4).

If there had been no exile, the Old Testament would never have handed on to us these words so vibrant with God's love. If there had been no cross, we would never have glimpsed the infinitely human depth of God's love. Why are we most deeply attached to people or to a cause for which we have suffered? Because, in some mysterious way, through suffering we have given the best of ourselves with no thought of reward. God gives to us, and we give to the world in need of salvation—and in a way to the Church that gave us birth—the same gift of love ratified by suffering. This is the key to the significance of blood in the working out of our redemption. Blood represents the most intimate, interior life, so much so that primitive mentalities identify blood with life itself. The value of blood and the value of a person are equally beyond all calculation. "You must be scrupulously careful as long as you are living away from your home.... Remember, the ransom that was paid to free you...was not paid in anything corruptible, neither in silver nor gold, but in the precious blood of a lamb without spot or stain, namely Christ" (1 Pt 1:17-19). The cross is therefore the true fulfillment of the first pasch, and Jesus is the true lamb. In him God saves us no longer by exterior events but by giving himself personally. This is the personal, inner ratification of the covenant that transforms our whole life: "And I live now not with my own life but with the life of Christ who lives in me. The life I now live in this body I live in faith: faith in the Son of God who loved me and sacrificed himself for my sake" (Gal 2:20).

In reality, the son who dies on the cross is not only he who became "completely like his brothers" in order to champion them (Heb 2:16-17); he is also the living God in whom death becomes resurrection. Through him the cross becomes the Tree of Life. Jesus crucified is our resurrection, the stream of life in which mercy flows into the roots of the world, restoring it to life. "By God's grace he had to experience death for all mankind" (Heb 2:9).

This is the ultimate in God's pedagogical method, and it is not the least disconcerting for human wisdom. God's life-giving power is revealed in his vulnerability. The violence of sin and death are vanquished by the non-violence of love. The cross is the calm of victory won by the gentleness of the word: the dying Christ expresses only consent. And this is why, in a new and eternal covenant, he is the word that brings creation to fulfillment as well as the man who consents, at last, to be created in love. The word and man's response are united in one filial offering to the Father. An attitude of self-oblation is well-nigh impossible for us, but Jesus lives it in infinite gratuitousness. Because he is utterly given, he absorbs death by allowing himself to fall into its clutches. The unconditional assent of the incarnate word, as he dies on the cross, deadens the sting of death forever. The resistance offered by our pride is finally broken; our aggressiveness subsides, disarmed. Jesus' vulnerability reveals God's real weakness: Love possesses nothing, it is everything. Herein lies its strength.

"The disciple that Jesus loved" contemplated his glory when he was raised up on the cross (Jn 1:14; 19:37), for the resurrection takes place on the cross. In this act, creation that has been "deprived of God's glory" is definitively set on a new path, and God's wisdom and power and his holiness that makes all things holy are made manifest (Rom 3:24-26; 1 Cor 1). The power of the cross is that in Jesus' wounds we find healing (1 Pt 2:24; Is 53:5).

Through the wound that our sin has opened in his body, his grace can at last flow into us. It is the only opening by which prideful man can reach salvation, just as punishment is in the end the only manifestation of God's love to which the hardened sinner can respond. The wonderful power of Jesus crucified is the power to make hearts of stone accessible to love. When he gives up his spirit on the cross, he pours out the Holy Spirit into our hearts, born to new life (Ez 36:26).

The covenant is God's gift to man. The cross is the super-abundance of this giving—his forgiving—and it overcomes all the obstacles we raise in the path of his giving. How different this is from our own petty accounting. We only remit a debt if it is useful for us to so. Jesus expressed magnanimity by his whole life. We have only to see with what infinite respect he treated sinners: Levi, the woman taken into adultery, the public sinner at Simon's dinner, Zacheus, Peter—they are all converted by his presence, recreated by his loving silence. On the cross the word is present to his executioners, and his love reaches out to recreate them and each one of us: "Father, forgive them" (Lk 23:24; 1 Pt 2:23). We need to learn how to speak of God before we can speak of others: the mystery, the silence and the love are the same.

God's wound becomes ours on the cross. The exile was the first step in the punishment foretold by the Prophets, and Jesus lives it out to the bitter end. God's anger is only the last resort of love which has no recourse other than to save us through suffering, and Jesus bears the weight of this love-suffering and brings it to perfection for the salvation of the world. In his person the suffering that is felt in the hearts of sinners becomes the pain that opens them to repentance and love. "I am the one who reproves and disciplines all those he loves" (Rv 3:19; Prv 3:12). In Jesus we are "reproved" and brought back to the Father in an attitude of filial simplicity. In his blood we have access to the Father (Heb 10:19). This is the new way that brings the long trail of exile to an end: everything converges in this one gesture of turning back to the Father (Lk 15:20).

And so the cross is the fulfillment of the exile. Just when everything seems to be lost, everything is renewed. We must lose everything in order to find everything in him: "If anyone wants to be a follower of mine, let him renounce himself and take up his cross and follow me. For anyone who wants to save his life will lose it: but anyone who loses his life for my sake, and for the sake of the Gospel, will save it" (Mk 8:34-35). The promised land seemed lost beyond recall: "Today you will be with me in Paradise" (Lk 23:45). The nation was scattered: Jesus dies "not for the nation only, but to gather together in unity the scattered children of God" (Jn 11:52). The Holy City was laid waste: "The throne of God and of the Lamb will be in its place in the city" (Rv 22:3). The temple was falling into ruin: "Destroy this sanctuary and in three days I will raise it up" (Jn 2:19). God's glory dwelt no longer in the tabernacle: "Father, the hour has come: glorify your Son" (Jn 17:2).

The fruit of the cross, prefigured in the deportation, is the inner fulfillment of God's pasch in men. The uncompromising holiness of the living God enters the heart of man through the crucified Christ. It is on the cross that the word is revealed as "something alive and active: it cuts like any double-edged sword but more finely; it can slip through the place where the soul is divided from the spirit" (Heb 4:12). And this life-giving energy manifested in Christ's death on the cross is the undying fidelity of God's love. We only really know someone's love when we have been forgiven. We only know the overwhelming truth of God's love in the forgiveness he holds out to us every day of our lives. And the wonderful thing is that after forgiveness, life flows more strongly than ever: "No need to recall the past.... See, I am doing a new deed" (Is 43:18-19). The exile is an absence which restores, later, an even deeper presence. This is what is suggested by the successive awakening of the Spouse in the Song of Songs. God, in his fidelity, cannot find it in his heart to envisage an exile that will not be followed by a home-coming.

CHAPTER NINE

The Homecoming, the Mediation of Love

We have seen that we really only know how much a person loves us when we have experienced his forgiveness, and that this is especially true where God is concerned. We must also add that we, in turn, express the best of our love when we forgive. Forgiveness is the self-giving that reaches out beyond all barriers and limitations. It is the total gratuitousness that breaks down the resistance of a hard and narrow heart making it capable of opening out in welcome. The very resistance we offer and the pettiness of our hearts reveal the gratuitousness of God's giving and forgiving. The resistance and pettiness we meet with in others should stimulate gratuitousness in us. The darkness of the period of exile—our own sin—comes to an end in this new dawn. We cannot stay far from others' indefinitely, any more than we can stay far from God. The possibility of conversion is constantly before us, just as it is always possible to reconcile ourselves with our fellows. This is the drama of all

207

homecomings, the drama of the mediation of love.

Our journey on this earth is an apprenticeship of life, and the time of exile is the school. Many prisoners of war could bear witness to the fact that in prison one discovers inner ways hitherto unknown. They are the ways of love as it becomes more human and more realistic. The full development of our personal maturity and our capacity to live harmoniously in society requires that we free ourselves from our last bonds, and we can only do so if we touch rock bottom. This is what Christ did, with us and for us. In his mysterious "descent into Hell" he plumbed the depth of our mortal condition and brought light into its darkest corners. "The people that walked in darkness has seen a great light," "a light that darkness could not overpower" (Is 9:1; Jn 1:5). What are these new glimmerings of light that become visible in the course of our second exodus?

The Prophets of the sixth century B.C. and especially Isaiah describe the return from exile as a second exodus. They see it as a growth in maturity in two aspects that cannot be dissociated. The first: the necessarily personal, inner nature of our living for God; the second: the cohesion of God's people moving from a purely tribal solidarity to become a living community. To reach maturity and break through the darkness of sin we must meet these demands in our own lives and arrive at a more vigorous, personal spiritual life and a deeper-seated solidarity with our fellows. This is what it means to live the mystery of the Church on the level of the Spirit and of Christ's body, and this is how the covenant and the kingdom grow in our lives. The kingdom on the level of the Spirit is the community of the poor in spirit incarnate in the Church. On the level of Christ's body, it is the ecclesial community animated by the Spirit. The mediation of love has to be lived out concretely by mature members of the Church rooted in the Spirit and incarnate in the human community. This is the mediation of Christ by which God saves the world through the work of man.

And so this twin axis of growth is really one: a presence lived on a deeper level. The exile of sin opens our inner being to God and to our fellows in greater humility and greater love. Nothing can make us more jubilantly aware of the presence of one we love than an experience of his absence. The forgiveness of sin is this wonderful rediscovery. It is a renewal in which we discover the secret paths of true love: "No need to recall the past, no need to think about what was done before. See, I am doing a new deed, even now it comes to light; can you not see it?" (Is 43:18-19).

THE COMMUNITY OF THE POOR IN SPIRIT

When our Lord proclaims the charter of the Good News, the first qualification he requires, and which sums up the new life, is that we be poor in spirit. A heart dispossessed of itself and of all attachment to material belongings, a heart that lies open to others in an attitude of oblation is a heart in which the spirit is at work. It is the Spirit who is revealed in exile. The nation has been cut off from all economic and political power and has tasted the emptiness of its own self-sufficiency and has thus become capable of breathing the more rarefied air of the Spirit. The principle prophecies of Jeremiah and Ezekiel concern this renewal in the Spirit. Deprived of all psychological props and formalistic observances, Israel is free to discover that the true vitality of God and man are joined in the inner life of the Spirit. In a man's heart poverty is, as it were, the hollow that God's love comes to fill. "Deep within them I will plan my Law, writing it on their hearts" (Jer 31:33). When Jesus comes to give the new Spirit, he must be greeted by hearts purified by the experience of a return from exile. To be poor in spirit supposes a change of heart.

A contrite heart. The period after a war is propitious, especially for those who have lost, for examination of conscience, reappraisal, regret and reconciliation. In its own way Israel underwent a period of "revival" in a spirit of deeper interiority when it returned from exile. The Deuteronomic prophets had always insisted upon the need for a change of heart, but the story of Jeremiah's tribulations is enough to show that their teaching had never really been assimilated. A salutary experience of suffering was needed to bring this home to the people. The faithful remnant of Israel that returns to Palestine has at last understood. The post-exilic writings of the end of the sixth century B.C. and those of the terrible period of Syrian persecution in the second century are characterized by the spirit of repentance and of conversion. Here we find the first examples of a penitential liturgy which the Christian tradition received from the synagogue and the Temple. (See Neh 9; Is 58; 63:7–64:11; Pss 51; 79; 106; Jl 1–2; Dn 9:4-19; Bar 1:15–3:8.)

In the conversion of heart can be seen the first signs of the mediation of renewed love. The first movement is one of truth, in which we recognize our fault for what it is: "Father, I have sinned against heaven and against you" (Lk 15:18-21). A change of heart begins in the recognition that we have been wanting in love toward our God ("heaven") and toward our fellows ("you"). This is the first meaning of the word "confession": it is a recognition which begins in truth and ends in joy (Lk 15:22-32).

But it is not simply a recognition of something within ourselves. More fundamentally it is a recognition of the One who loves us: "If you wish to come back, Israel—it is Yahweh who speaks—it is to me you must return" (Jer 4:1). Confession can never be simply a list of breaches of a law, it is essentially an opening to a presence. The most beautiful passages of the Old Testament about repentance are always in the form of a dialogue with God. A man does not confess his sin to himself but to God, unfolding it to the light of his countenance. What is more, it is not a question simply of admitting one's infidelities, it is a question of weaving them back into the fabric of his fidelity. In the liturgy of the ninth chapter of Nehemiah, in Psalm 106, in Daniel's solitary prayer (Dn 9:1-19) and in the community confession of sin described in Baruch (Bar 1:15-3:8), the whole history of the wonderful works that Yahweh has wrought for his people is called to mind. To recognize that one is a sinner is to confess one's sin and, in the same movement, to confess God's unfailing love. These are the two faces of one coin, the coin of grateful recognition. This is very different from the feelings of contrition that we sometimes try to wring from a withered heart. A truly contrite heart is a heart crushed not by remorse but by love.

It is precisely because a contrite heart is moved by love that it can change and turn back. The contrition taught by the gospel is born of gratitude, and it matures in conversion.

The penitential liturgies express a will to change, to be quit of the estrangement of exile and return home to the Father. Here too it is not a self-contained autodynamic movement. The conversion taught by the gospel is not the same as the self-sufficient autonomy of the stoics or ancient sages. It is an event that we live in the covenant that is established between us and God. It is not a psychological or moral maneuver, it is someone: Jesus Christ. When Jesus announces the good news already foretold by Isaiah (chap. 40), he can in all truth say, "Repent, and believe the Good News" (Mk 1:15), because in him, personally "the Kingdom of God is close at hand." Jesus is the living path to conversion because he is our return to the Father. In him our will to change finds its true accents; it is founded not on the presumptuous self-reliance of before the exile but on his unwavering fidelity. The will of repentance is humble and audacious, for it springs from the gift of the Spirit. Christ has become our reconciliation. "It is all God's work. It was God who reconciled us to himself through Christ . . . be reconciled to God. For our sake God make the sinless one into sin, so that in him we might become the goodness of God" (2 Cor 5:18-21).

The covenant reaches such depths in this path of return that everything comes from God. And yet God can do nothing if we are not wholehearted in our intention: "Bring me back, let me come back, for you are Yahweh my God" (Jer 31:18). "What am I to do with you Judah? This love of yours is like a morning cloud, like the dew that quickly disappears" (Hos 6:4). "Turn again, then, to your God, hold fast to love and justice, and always put your trust in your God"

(Hos 12:7). The period of exile forges a true hope very different to a wishful passivity, so that when we set out on the path that leads to home it is because we truly want to, and yet it is God's freely given love that moves us. "It is God, for his own loving purpose, who puts both the will and the action into you" (Phil 2:13). "I have dispelled your faults like a cloud, your sins like a mist. Come back to me, for I have redeemed you" (Is 44:22). The reconciliation that God effects with us is not a legal artifice. Within the covenant written in our hearts, our source is both God and ourselves, our return to him is both his act and ours. And as the Spirit is our source, he is also our remission of sin: "Receive the Holy Spirit. For those whose sins you forgive they are forgiven" (Jn 20:22-23).

The gift of the Spirit brings with it the kingdom with its inexhaustible treasure of "Good News." "Happy are the poor in spirit; theirs is the kingdom of heaven" (Mt 5:3). God requires only one condition preliminary to this gift, one attitude that will mediate this plentitude: to be poor. The kingdom is God himself who comes to us through Christ in his Spirit, and the only spiritual problem we have to face is how to receive God. "There is no need to be afraid, little flock, for it has pleased your Father to give you the Kingdom" (Lk 12:32), "But the remnant of my flock I myself will gather from all the countries where I have dispersed them, and will bring them back to their pastures...no fear, no terror for them any more; not one shall be lost" (Jer 23:3-4). The faithful remnant, the little flock, the community of the poor in heart; this is what we must be if we are to have our part in the new covenant established by Christ.

We recognize here the paradoxical message of the whole gospel: if you want to be filled with the richness of God, you must be poor; if you want to possess all, you must possess nothing. It is the same paradox of the pasch that becomes interior to each man in the period of exile: we must die in order to live. This paradox is the wonderful way God found to be with each one of us in our personal life story and by which he causes suffering, which is evil and the fruit of sin but which cannot simply be destroyed, to become the seed of salvation. In Christ, suffering is no longer a wall that closes us off from God and other people but a door opening on to them.

All this is very disconcerting to our human wisdom. We would never have arranged things this way. But to enable us to live in this climate, God has spoken to us, not in stirring speeches—one cannot talk of suffering, it can only be lived— but in facts. We can see the expression of the suffering of the poor in spirit in the Old Testament stories of Samuel's mother, Hannah (1 Sm 1:1–2:11), of David (2 Sm 22), of Jeremiah (Jer 15:10-30; 18:18 f; 20:7 f) and the suffering servant of Yahweh (Is 52:13-53), and especially in the Psalms that express the sufferings of the poor, victims of oppression by the rich. In the Psalms poverty becomes, progressively, an expansion of the heart to the point where Christ uses the words of the Psalms to express his own drama in his crucifixion and resurrection (Mt 27:46). At the end of the long line of lowly saints of the Old Testament who lived wholly for God, Christ is the truly poor man whose being is filled with the fullness of God. "What is good has been explained to you, man; this is what Yahweh asks of you: only this, to act justly, to love tenderly and to walk humbly with your God" (Mi 6:8).

But the man Jesus was brought up by someone, someone in whom the salvation he brought with him to the world reached perfection: his mother. The Virgin Mary is the one person who has lived the poverty of the gospel with the whole of her being. What is the message that lies in this mystery of the Church? What does it hold for us, this silent mystery of Our Lady's life? It is that to be poor in heart is to be filled with God's infinite presence and to realize that he is all, that he is God and not man. It is to believe wholeheartedly that he is love and that love is supreme. And this is why Our Lady is an almost silent figure. For she lives in a silence attentive to God and to God alone, adoring him ceaselessly in the admiration of love. The very breath of a soul that is a silent prayer, for it is wrapped in the mantle of God's presence and lives for him alone.

If we are poor we know what it means to be hungry. A soul that is poor is hungry and thirsty for God. "Oh, come to the water all you who are thirsty; though you have no money, come! Why spend money on what is not bread, your wages on what fails to satisfy?" (Is 55:1-2). Real hunger cannot be satisfied with trivialities disguised as love: they only leave us empty and with a taste of nothingness. Only God is the plentitude that gives himself by drawing us to himself and satisfies our hunger by making us forever hunger for him.

The poverty given by the Spirit is a permanent capacity for openness. The Virgin Mary, the Church, the poor in spirit consent to be saved at every moment. "Anyone who does not welcome the Kingdom of God like a little child will never enter it" (Mk 10:15). If the Spirit lives in us we recognize our Father, and we learn that the characteristic of love is self-giving. One who is poor in spirit seeks to live within the source so that he may be wholly a gift of God, absolute gratuitousness, merciful love. Once a heart is transparently open to God's gift, all is a gift.

One who is poor according to the Spirit bathes in God's light. There is no more darkness in him (1 Jn 1:5-7). He is humble, uncompromisingly true, with no illusions about himself or others and with no bitterness. He is in peace. What more peaceful freedom could be attained (Jn 8:32) than to love what is true (1 Jn 5:20)? Because he sees himself and God in the same light of truth he can live, in the will of God whom he loves, in the midst of consuming activity. A heart that is poor knows how to wait: when God gives himself, he places us in an attitude of waiting.

This is the key to the extremely realistic nature of evangelical poverty of heart: one is no longer astonished at his own weakness or failures. Are we capable, of ourselves, of doing more than stumble along God's ways? Every form of resentment or discouragement, of presumptuousness or vanity is killed at its roots. The poor man can no longer accept his own pretences at their face value, he has a pronounced taste for authenticity: "Seek Yahweh, all you, the humble of the earth, who obey his commands. Seek integrity, seek humility" (Zep 2:3).

The more a person develops a capacity for love the more he is able to suffer. This is the way of suffering accepted by the Virgin Mary (Lk 2:35) and by the Church (Mt 24:8-13). We can see this in our own mothers: when life has given them a deep capacity for suffering and love, they become interiorly silent. They seem to see into the inner depths of people and events. Someone who is really poor is one in whom suffering has bestowed a quality of sweetness and peace that affects all who come into contact with him. He has learned through his suffering—or rather from Christ, the model of poverty—what it means to love, so that he knows, understands and forgives everything. And, above all, someone who is poor is ingenious, discrete and self-effacing in finding ways to bathe the wounds of others in a sweetness that heals them and sets them free (1 Cor 13:3; Gal 5:22-25).

The poor man, being dispossessed of self, is flexible in the hands of God and available and dedicated to others. Generously and tirelessly he strives to overcome the obstacles to love, for God's strength dwells in him. In the apostles' first preaching, as told in the Acts of the Apostles, Jesus is spoken of as the poor servant through whom God performs the work of salvation in power. This is the experience, in Christ, of every baptized person: "I shall be very happy to make my weaknesses my special boast so that the power of Christ may stay over me…for it is when I am weak that I am strong" (2 Cor 12:9-10). The whole feeling that pervades this chapter of the Second Letter to the Corinthians is the same that one finds in the Song of Moses after the liberation from Egypt and in the Song of Hannah at the birth of Samuel. But its most perfect expression is in Mary's song, the Magnificat, when she meets Elizabeth. A poor heart is a heart full of song and exultation. When a person is filled with God's presence and transparently open to his grace how can he help but "leap for joy" (Lk 1:44)? This is the pervading climate of the true Christian community of the poor in spirit, born as they are of

217

the Lord Christ, the poor servant of God (Acts 4:23-35).

THE ECCLESIAL COMMUNITY

Jesus came to fulfill, not to destroy. The community of the poor of heart takes shape slowly in the centuries that divide the exile from the preaching of John the Baptist, and it reaches accomplishment in Christ, the Servant of Yahweh, and the faithful remnant that gathers round him. But there are other dimensions of the return from exile that Christ brings to fulfillment and that are closely related to the dimension of poverty, notably the ecclesial significance of the faithful remnant. The time of exile was not only a period of spiritual purification for God's people, it was also a time of apprenticeship in a new life-style. The true Judaism that Ezekiel and the post-exilic prophets envisage is the result both of a change of heart and of a change of structures. Ezekiel's "charter of Judaism" is too often seen to be contained only in chapters forty to forty-eight of the book of his prophecies as we have it today. In point of fact the first glimpse of a deep renewal can already be seen in chapter thirty-three, when Ezekiel is called a second time to a vocation. Chapters thirty-four to forty-eight form a coherent whole, outlining, first, the spiritual reform of the community returning to Palestine (chaps. 34–37); second, the apocalyptic struggle of the theocratic community (chaps. 38, 39); third, the structural reforms based on the City and the Temple (chaps. 40–48). The new Israel is seen in a dyptich—the spiritual and the structural reforms—hinging on the central axis of the struggle of the last days during which God's holiness will be revealed to all the nations. How is this fulfilled in

Christ and in the Church, God's "new Israel"? This is the mystery of the incarnation of the kingdom, the spiritual community of the poor in spirit in history and in human society: the two-fold dimension, historical and sociological, of the working of the Spirit in the Church, Body of Christ. It is the mystery of the new wine and the old wine-skins, of a new creation introduced by the Spirit of the risen Christ into the framework of the old creation destined to disintegrate. Christ's accomplishment is not that he establishes new structures to replace the old, but that he breathes into the simplified and purified structures the new breath of the Spirit which will remain for ever distinct from and uncontaminated by its containing structures: "You are in the world...you are not of the world."

THE HISTORICAL DIMENSION OR THE CHURCH SEEN AS AN APOCALYPTIC COMMUNITY

It is interesting to note that Israel began to realize its identity as an ecclesial community at the same time and for the same reasons it began to realize it could never be just one amongst the other religious and political communities that surrounded it. It is true that the notion of being a chosen people, set apart and holy, was familiar to the Jews from the time of Moses and had been taught by all their teachers and prophets, but as we have seen, this "priestly" people had succumbed to the temptation of being great in the temporal order. Their return from exile, led by the priests and scribes, was at the same time an expression of a will to return in fidelity to their origins. Their resistance of a political structuration and their refusal to align themselves with the rival power blocs of East and West nearly caused them to be completely wiped out. And the ambiguity of the reaction led by the Maccabees lay in the refusal to make peace with the Hellenic neo-pagan powers while at the same time giving tacit consent to their methods. Finally secularization leads to the corruption of the whole system, including the royal establishment and the priesthood. The epilogue to this is the destruction of the Jewish ecclesial community provoked by the fanatical resistance of the Pharisees and zealots who had recourse to the enemies' own methods: war and violence. The People of God, even under the old disposition, is always overcome by "the world" as soon as it consents to be "of" the world.

The precarious and uneasy existence of God's kingdom in this world helps us understand why the period of the return was so rich in apocalyptic literature. Some forerunners, although of a very different style, can be seen in the pre-exilic prophets in their "oracles against the (pagan) nations." A large section of Ezekiel is dedicated to the same theme (chaps. 25–32). But the apocalypse of chapters thirty-eight and thirty-nine opens up entirely new perspectives to the people: the conflict between the spiritual community and the pagan nations will grow in intensity and will serve both to purify God's people and to bear witness to the Lord in the face of all nations. Once a faithful remnant accepts to live solely for God, a witness to the true God is given and the judgment of the world has begun. This is a new departure in the notion of salvation: henceforth the pasch of the Lord is seen to be advancing inexorably toward the culminating point that will bring a total and universal liberation, even to the world of inanimate beings.

The dichotomy underlying all apocalyptic texts of both testaments is expressed in various ways. In Ezekiel, Isaiah, Zechariah and Daniel the opposition is portrayed as being between the People of God and the "Nations." In the Psalms it is seen as the opposition between God's poor on the one hand and the "enemies" on the other, or between the "inhabitants of the earth" (the present-people) and the "rich." In the New Testament the real conflict becomes clear and is brought to a head: it is the conflict between the Son of God and "the Tempter," between the Son of Man and the "Prince of this world," between Light and Darkness, Truth and Lies, Life and Death. And, when referring to the Church, the conflict is seen to oppose the "children of God" and "the world," the "children of light" and the "children of darkness," the woman and the dragon, the "offspring of the woman" and the "offspring of the serpent." Paul expresses this apocalyptic and eschatological reality in terms of our personal conflict. He speaks of the "spirit" that wars against the "flesh," of the "new man" and the "old man." And speaking of the newness that Christ has brought into the world, he talks of a conflict between the "time to come" and the "present time." The first chapter of the Letter to the Thessalonians and the letters written in captivity speak of the personal drama of every Christian, as well as that of the Church, as the struggle that will "reveal" God's coming in power (apocalypse) because we have, in Christ, already entered into the "last days" (eschatology).

It is essential to our understanding of the relation between structures and spirit in the Church today that we grasp the importance of the apocalyptic struggle portrayed in Ezekiel and Revelation. Upon it hinges the right balance between the spiritual and the incarnate aspects of God's new people. Both of these aspects are necessary. Christ's body cannot live without his Spirit, and a purely spiritual community cannot exist without an incarnation in structures. But each is in relation to the other: the ecclesial is in the service of the spiritual, faith and hope and all that expresses them are in the service of charity. The particular forms in which faith, hope and charity are incarnate are necessary but transitory. And this is why the apocalyptic combat is inherent in all Christian experience of love. The divine life must permeate all our structures, from the psychological to the economic. This is our constant task, and at the same time we have to be constantly on guard against the danger of identifying the divine life with the structures that contain it. If the yeast is really going to make the dough rise it must be of another nature, and it must be thoroughly blended into the dough. Personal purification and reform of the Church are two coordinate parts that must be inseparably present in the Christian experience. Neither one nor the other consists in the elimination of one of the poles of conflict, whether by dissolving into a purely spiritual community as though freed from all "impurities," or by hardening into absolute structures as though they were the new life of the Spirit.

And so if we place chapters thirty-eight and thirty-nine of Ezekiel into the wider framework of the apocalyptic writings of the Bible, we can learn a great deal about our present Christian condition. Some people always tend to "judaize" (Gal 2:14) in an attempt to establish a measurable norm, whether it be on a personal level by a presumptuous legalism or on a community level by clerical triumphalism. Others, whether in reaction to the former tendency or by the natural inclination, tend to "Hellenize" in search of a more down-to-earth wisdom that would eliminate the realism and the humility of the incarnation. But the Christian condition, both of individuals and of the community as a whole, is apocalyptic, torn in two like the crucified Christ, the power and the wisdom of God (1 Cor 1:17–2:6).

We have seen that the incarnation of love in our lives is a crucifixion. We can now try to see in what way it can truly be said to be an incarnation.

THE SOCIOLOGICAL DIMENSIONS OR THE CHURCH SEEN AS AN ECCLESIAL COMMUNITY

It has been said that the Messiah of the Book of Ezekiel is the Temple, and St. John, who was strongly influenced by this prophet of the captivity, takes up this theme. When we were speaking of the revelation of the kingdom, we saw how the specific characteristic of the People of God was to be a "royal priesthood." This priestly reality of holy consecration had already conferred upon the institution of Israel a character which made it impossible for them to see it as a purely political phenomenon long before the Babylonian captivity. The progress seen in the return from exile lies in the same direction. The veritable "mediations" of salvation can be seen more clearly. Just as poverty is the spiritual quality which reaches fulfillment in faith in Christ, so the purified

sacerdotal structures of the Jewish community reach fulfillment, in Christ, in the human dimension of the Church.

We cannot understand this properly if we see what is
accomplished in Christ as simply the logical fulfillment of the
old order. It is exactly the other way round, and the earliest
preaching of the apostles shows that they were aware of this.
Jesus of Nazareth, risen from the dead, is their starting point,
and taking up the Baptist's teaching to the first community of
the poor, they show that it is he who is the Christ, the faithful
servant of Yahweh. In Jesus they find the accomplishment of
the three great mediations prefigured in the Old Law. Jesus
is the Prophet, the new Moses; he is the son of David, true
king and shepherd of his flock; he is the Temple, the Paschal
Lamb and the eternal High Priest according to the order of
Melchisedech. And each one of these three mediations
reaches fulfillment in the central figure that reveals the true
visage of Christ, the suffering and glorified servant of
Yahweh (Is 42:1-9; 49:1-6; 50:4-11; 52:13; 53:12; Jn 1:29-34;
Acts 4:23-30; Phil 2:6-11).

The Jews and the Greeks both failed to accept this
mystery of Jesus-mediator and failed, therefore, like the
other "rulers of the world," to recognize the Lord of Glory (1
Cor 2:1-9). The Church, like its Lord, is essentially a ministry,
a servant (Lk 22:24-32; Jn 13:1-20). The fact that we are sent
into the world as prophets, priests and shepherds—in other
words that the Magisterium, orders and jurisdiction are the
charismata of the ecclesial community—means, on the one
hand, that these functions are directed to a service ("serve
one another, rather, in the words of love" Gal 5:13) and, on
the other hand, that the structural aspect is not subject to

purely sociological norms. The ecclesial reality can be studied by religious sociology, but its deep nature is of quite another order. The social structures of the Church of Christ are charismatic by nature (1 Cor 12; Eph 4:1-16). They are gifts of the Spirit for the service of the body, talents entrusted to the servants of Christ by which they have to build up his body with living stones. The mission is not a question of proselytism, any more than Christian instruction is a question of commercial publicity.

And so the return from exile, in God's plan, reveals both the basic tension of our Christian experience and our mission in the world. This is what it means to live "in Christ" in the fullest sense of mediation that Paul attributes to this expression. But we must go farther in our understanding of the accomplishment wrought by Christ. Two texts of St. Paul are instructive: 1 Corinthians 11:2-12 and Ephesians 5:23-32. These are the passages in which he uses the nuptial image used by the Prophets and Song of Songs to speak of the relations between God and humanity, basing his teaching on the relationship between man and woman. This theme is accomplished in Christ and the Church. And at this point we can see the truth of the incarnation in another light. Although Christ is our homecoming, we still have to come home. The Song of Songs reiterates the successive "returns" that build up to the final return of God's people from exile. Jesus is the only mediator between God and man, but since he is "one flesh" with his Church, the Church follows where he goes, and in him the Church is mediator. And this is why every human being, whether man or woman, who lives in Christ is entrusted with a charism of mediation and of service. At the same time, within Christ and his Church the complementarity of men and women subsists. The same breath of the same Spirit gives life to a masculine charism and to a feminine charism. Paul does not neglect to remind us of this when he speaks of marriage and of the veil that women should wear in the assemblies of the pastoral organization of the nascent churches (1 Cor 11:2-16; 14:33-40).

According to the first experience of the Church, it would seem that the prophetic, sacerdotal and pastoral charismata, in their structural dimension, are reserved to men. Men fulfill their functional vocation in Christ, "savior of the Body," spouse of the Church. Some of the extreme positions held by feminists end by denying all true originality to women in an attempt to make them absolutely equal to men. And, in some Churches, ministries which have been traditionally reserved to men are now being conferred on women. However, the arguments based on psychological reasons which are used to oppose the admission of women to the ordained ministry do not seem to be conclusive. Since it is equally a question of the service of the Church—and not only of the subjects concerned—specific and formal arguments should also follow from the nature of the Church. And it seems that Christ's mystery of union with his Church, symbolized and accomplished in the union of man and woman, is the basis for the specific, functional vocation of men and women within the Church. From the viewpoint of their own particular and original charismata, man lives more by Christ, woman more by the Church. At the same time, of course, from the viewpoint of the divine life within them they both live by Christ and by the Church.

It is not a question of women being in any way infe-
rior to men. Quite the contrary. The first source of the liberation of womankind in history was the Virgin Mary. She was
the first to live "in the fullness" of grace (Lk 1:28), the mystery of the Church—spouse, virgin and mother—saved by
Christ. The later books of the Old Testament and many passages in the New allude to a salvation wrought by the woman
in exact parallel to the ancient tradition of the fall caused by
the woman. The Book of Ruth, the Song of Songs, the Books
of Esther and Judith not to mention the allegories of the wisdom books (Prv 9:1-6; Sir 24; Bar 3:9–5:9; Tb 13) as well as
the letters of Paul, the Gospels of Luke and John and especially the Book of Revelation all see in the mystery of the
woman and the Church the mystery of humanity associated
with God in the work of its own salvation. Every member of
the Body of Christ participates in the nuptial, virginal and
maternal mystery of the Church, and each in his own way
according to the charismata given by the Spirit. From this
viewpoint one might say that the charismata proper to men
seem to stand more in relation to the ecclesial and structural
aspects of the Church whereas those of women seem to be
more in relation to the spiritual and interior aspects. But in
the last analysis "though women cannot do without man, neither can man do without woman, in the lord; woman may
come from man, but man is born of woman—both come from
God" (1 Cor 11:11-12).

CHAPTER TEN

The Resurrection, the Victory of Love

After the return from captivity in Babylon there was an attempt at a restoration. It was an attempt at a new style of community stripped of all ambitions of conquest and centered on the coming of the reign of Yahweh amongst his own people and through the universe. The result of this attempt was both failure and success. It was a failure insofar as it was still concerned with temporal, political, racial or legal considerations. It was a success insofar as it was a community of the faithful remnant of God's poor that reached fulfillment in Mary, in Christ and in his first disciples. We can now try and see in what way the restoration undertaken at the end of the sixth century is finally brought to fulfillment in Christ.

God's plan for the world has never been advanced by spectacular events (Mt 4:1-11). Even when the fullness of time was accomplished in the person of Jesus, it began in obscurity, like all the beginnings of life. And Jesus remained hidden from the public eye for thirty years, learning to live

with other men instead of trying ingenuously to impose salvation on them from outside, as so many international
"experts" attempt to do today. Then, when he knew their life
as one of them and spoke their language, he revealed to those
around him the novelty of the kingdom that he brought with
him. He begins with a slow, progressive revelation which ultimately fails to penetrate the hearts of these "natural" men,
and so he goes farther afield and allows himself to be led to
the ultimate limits of absurdity of the human condition:
death. But the word of God is not just someone who teaches
us about life, he is the Living One who gives life. In taking on
the whole of the human condition, he brings man to fulfillment on his own, divine level. The universal restoration
glimpsed by the prophets and apocalyptic writers of the last
centuries before Christ is not a restoration of doctrine or of
structures; it is the event of the word of God and his personal
life in which are caught up and fulfilled every other personal
being and the cosmos itself. The true restoration is inaugurated on Easter morning, the first day of the new creation, the
true "Day of the Lord" that has been so long in coming. But
now it has come it will know no decline.

In the light of the resurrection, history can be seen
as God's great paschal design, the design that calls for the
progressive personalization and divinization of all beings created in the likeness of God-Love, all "recapitulated" in the
son. The Christian experience is essentially the experience of
the risen Christ. In him history is really renewed with the
novelty that resides in the gospel. In him we can grasp the
beginning and the end of all things: "he who has been initiated into the hidden power of the Resurrection knows for

what purposes God predisposed the beginning of all things" (Maximus the Confessor). To experience Christ, crucified and risen, is to discover the mysterious plan that has been entrusted to us and in which all individual paths, historical and spiritual, are included: a person is at the origin of all light; a gift of love is at the origin of all movement of life; and all things reach their final perfection by striving toward this personal source of light and love. The aspiration of every creature toward that personal communion—"show me your face"—is fulfilled in the risen Christ. He illuminates all things with the light of God's countenance, and in him all things are filled with God's presence. The risen Christ ushers in the fullness of God, "all things to all men." In him we can actually experience the union of everything human, of everything created, with the living God. The risen Christ is the final victory of love over every form of death. He is a human person who at last reaches liberation in the perfect harmony of communion. In order to get to know him better through the Bible, we shall now attempt to have a clearer view of who this person is who rose from the dead and the nature of this radical renewal that he brings into the world.

THE RISEN CHRIST

To know Christ Jesus in all truth, we must see him living. Someone who lives is not of the past but of the present; he is today. Love requires a presence. "The love of Christ overwhelms us when we reflect that if one man died for all, then all men should be dead; and the reason he died for all was so that living men should live no longer for themselves, but for him who died and was raised to life for them. From now onward, therefore, we do not judge anyone by the standards of the flesh. Even if we did once know Christ in the flesh, that is not how we know him now. And for anyone who is in Christ there is a new creation; the old creation has gone, and now the new one is here" (2 Cor 5:14-17).

If we are really to know Christ, therefore, we have to enter into him and into a new life. We know him when we have an actual and personal experience of his vivifying action. "The first man, Adam, as Scripture says, became a living soul"—and we in turn have received this from him when we have received our being—"but the last Adam has become a life-giving spirit"—and this we have still to receive from him in order to become fully ourselves (1 Cor 15:45-49). And so we live in him when we have effectively gone beyond every form of death: isolation in sin, destructive forms of suffering, hate and opposition to others and finally the destruction of our mortal bodies. Jesus, risen from the dead, is the body of man that has fallen like a seed into the ground and now bears fruit of eternal life. The life that is love and has flooded with the sap of life the stem and branches of his spiritual being as well as the bark of his corporeal existence. The whole of his being has become a transparent openness to communion. When we exist in him, we also become gradually simpler in the same transparency. Our bodily death will be the final step in this process.

"To know Christ and the power of his resurrection" (Phil 3:10-11) means, therefore, to get back into the original stream of life in which we can bring to their proper fulfillment all the incoherent, halting movements of our deepest being which is still so lost in its own complexity. This is the power of the life-stream that flows from the cross. Only the searing experience of the cross is capable of gently uncovering the fires of love that smolder deep within us. And this is because the fountainhead of love lies deeper within us than even these incoherent yearnings. And so when we experience the power of the cross, we are born at last to our own liberated being freely offered and given to us because we are born to the One who frees us and who is both gift and offering.

Without rhetorical exaggeration, Paul can call the risen Christ the "first-born of all creation" (Col 1:15) as though his existence in the resurrection were anterior to all being. The flow of time takes place in a fourth dimension: the dimension of our inner being. The risen Christ is anterior to our lives as men reborn to love since he is the interior source of that rebirth. He, in person, is the second and eternal creation which brings the first, fugitive creation to a new birth from within. In the first creation man was the climax; in the second creation he becomes the root and the source of a new departure.

The risen Christ, therefore, is the inexhaustible communion, God dwelling in men's hearts. The life-giving spirit is not a treasure to be guarded jealously but a flood-tide that sweeps all before it in renewal. Even the sense of human work finds its ultimate direction here. Instead of being something completely extraneous to our spiritual life—as we so often make it—it becomes the action of the Spirit at work in the cosmos in order to raise it from the dead, in order to bring it from the realm of "flesh and blood" into the kingdom of the promise, the kingdom of love (1 Cor 15:50). The Christian who lives in the risen Christ is at work on the Sabbath, on a Sabbath that knows no end (Jn 5:17-25).

In him we can also see a new and eternal solidarity built on love. Our earlier interdependence, inherited from the first Adam, makes us all heirs to the same indigence of love (Rom 3:23) and to the same servitudes on the biological and socio-psychological levels. We have already seen that the triumphant emergence of a human person at the highest level of life is an experience of love and grace. The risen Christ is the new beginning of all humanity, and he establishes men in a solidarity of communion. Wherever there is true love among men, God is there; the risen Lord is at work, not always fully visible but in the semi-hidden way of the road to Emmaus. So that even now he can judge the value of our acts by the consistency of his presence amongst us: "I tell you solemnly, in so far as you did this to one of the least of these brothers of mine, you did it to me" (Mt 25:40). There is no need to look for hidden metaphors or a juridical imputation in Jesus' words about the judgment, as though God had agreed on a conventional identification with each human being. We can take them quite literally. Once risen from the dead, Jesus is the only son who, mysteriously but really, gathers to himself all the scattered children of God. "Go and find the brothers, and tell them: I am ascending to my Father and your Father, to my God and your God" (Jn 20:17). Mary of Magdala, whose great love has earned her the role of apostle to the apostles, bears the message of a new brotherhood hidden like yeast in the dough of humanity. The risen Christ is the leaven that makes the whole mass of humanity rise and expand in the joy of personal communion. Whenever two human beings break through into a true love and fellowship, it is because they are sustained by the risen Christ.

This is why, ultimately, he is the fulfillment of the promise. Abraham was afforded a glimpse of a posterity and of a land. Jesus, risen from the tomb, is the "Yes" to all God's promises (Acts 13:26-37; 2 Cor 1:20). Both the posterity and the land of the promise are contained in him. The children of the promise are those who are born, not to a particular race or nation, but to the kingdom of love through the Spirit. The true land in which man yearns to live forever is that same love, namely, God who can be known, at last, in the wonder of this truth incarnate.

Everything that is set down in the Old Testament and everything in the world comes to life when seen in the light of his countenance. From the first untilled soil of creation to the seed of the promise, from the springtime of the pasch to the winter of the exile and the long awaited return, everything comes to fruition in the harvest of the resurrection. "Those who went sowing in tears now sing as they reap. They went away, went away weeping, carrying the seed; they come back, come back singing, carrying their sheaves" (Ps 126:5-6). Everything is brought to joyous fulfillment in the eternal youth of the resurrection because the first dark days of creation, the seeds of joy and the power of life were already secretly at work.

ALL NEWNESS

A Christian who has already some experience of life in the Spirit knows that he has embarked upon an endless spiritual adventure, that he has left a dull routine of life behind him for ever. Old age, with its absurd and deceitful power of death, is already behind him. To live Christ in the smallest details of one's daily life is an experience of inexhaustible youth, always new, never repetitive. For the spiritual man, youth is ahead of him because it is within him. No event in our lives escapes this fundamental renewal, and every problem, whether of one's own inner balance or of other people's happiness, can be faced in the same peaceful and creative spirit of optimism. Ceaselessly, untiringly, love is with us to re-create, pacify, simplify everything in light. St. Irenaeus of Lyons, speaking of the pages of the Gospel that tell of the coming of Christ, says, "everything is *new*: the Word disposes *anew* his coming in the flesh…all these texts speak to us of one God inaugurating a *new* economy of freedom for men by the *new* arrangement of his Son's coming . . . with him the Spirit acquires the habit of dwelling in mankind, of resting amongst men, of inhabiting the work of God's hand, carrying out the will of the Father in these men and *renewing* them, from their decrepitude, in the *newness* of Christ" (Irenaeus, *Contra Omnes Haereses*, Bk 3).

In a very concrete, practical way the resurrection in which we live is this eternal newness. It is not just something new in the sense of being recent, the latest event. In a civilization that moves so fast, what is new today is no longer new tomorrow. "Every living thing grows old like a garment, the age-old law is 'Death must be'" (Sir 14:17). "The heavens will vanish like smoke, the earth wear out like a garment, and its inhabitants die like vermin, but my salvation shall last for ever and my justice have no end" (Is 51:6). But Christ is new as a never-failing spring is new. He is new as an on-going birth-process or an admiring love that feeds on the constant discovery of new causes for admiration. He is, in person, essential, eternal and integral newness. It is impossible to express this mystery satisfactorily, and it is also impossible to express exactly how this newness becomes ours, just as it is impossible to encompass the action of the Spirit in a formula. But the Bible conveys some notion of it through a certain number of symbols. We cannot make an exhaustive study of all of them, but let us note some that are most characteristic of the newness of Christ.

Creation is renewed in Christ. "The hand of Yahweh has done this, the Holy One of Israel has created it" (Is 41:20). "Let the earth open for salvation to spring up. Let deliverance, too, bud forth which I, Yahweh, will create" (Is 45:8). Because he is the Redeemer, God brings to fulfillment the love that lies dormant in the first creation. "Now I am revealing new things to you, things hidden and unknown to you, created just now, this very moment" (Is 48:6), "for now your creator will be your husband, his name, Yahweh Sabaoth; your redeemer will be the Holy One of Israel, he is called the God of the whole earth" (Is 54:5). "And for anyone who is in Christ, there is a new creation; the old creation has gone, and now the new one is here" (2 Cor 5:17). "What matters is to become an altogether new creature" (Gal 6:15).

The new creation is a new *birth*. "Unless a man is born through water and the Spirit, he cannot enter the kingdom of God . . . unless a man is born from above [or: anew] he cannot see the kingdom of God" (Jn 3:5, 3). "It was for no reason except his own compassion that he saved us, by means of the cleansing water of rebirth and by renewing us with the Holy Spirit" (Ti 3:5). Water symbolizes the primeval, maternal element of creation. Here it becomes the sign of a new birth of spiritual man. "Blessed be God the Father of our Lord Jesus Christ, who in his great mercy has given us a new birth as his sons, by raising Jesus Christ from the dead, so that we have a sure hope and the promise of an inheritance that can never be spoilt or soiled and never fade away" (1 Pt 1:3). "Your new birth was not from any mortal seed but from the everlasting word of the living and eternal God" (1 Pt 1:23). We are reborn of the love of the Father, by the Word, in the Spirit—an unceasing resurrection by which we are "dead men brought back to life" (Rom 6:13).

Because we are new men we are given a new *name*. Our new name expresses, in a mysterious way, our eternal personality. "I will give them an everlasting name that shall never be effaced" (Is 56:5), "and you will be called by a new name, one which the mouth of Yahweh will confer...no longer are you to be named 'Forsaken,' nor your land 'Abandoned,' but you shall be called 'My Delight' and your land 'The Wedded'" (Is 62:2-5). "My servants are to be given a new name" (Is 65:15), "to those who prove victorious I will give...a stone with a new name written on it, known only to the man who receives it" (Rv 2:17); "I will inscribe on them the name of my God and the name of the city of my God, the new Jerusalem which comes down from my God in heaven, and my own new name as well" (Rv 3:12). Our new name is the name into which we are plunged in baptism, the name of God, Father, Son and Holy Spirit, communion of love. This is the name of the Father bestows on his anointed (Jn 17:11-12), who in turn bestow it on all who give him welcome (Jn 1:12).

"Next in my vision I saw Mount Zion, and standing on it a Lamb who had with him a hundred and forty-four thousand people, all with his name and his Father's name written on their foreheads" (Rv 14:1). Our new name will be the splendor of our eternal being: "The throne of God and of the Lamb will be in its place in the city; his servants will worship him, they will see him face to face, and his name will be written on their foreheads" (Rv 22:3-4).

The baptismal rite uses another biblical symbol of newness in Christ, that of the robe or *garment*. We are robed now in a presence: "All baptized in Christ, you have all clothed yourselves in Christ" (Gal 3:27). "Let your armour be the lord Jesus Christ" (Rom 13:14). "I exult for you in Yahweh, my soul rejoices in my God, for he has clothed me in the garments of salvation, he has wrapped me in the cloak of integrity, like a bridegroom wearing his wreath, like a bride adorned in her jewels" (Is 61:10). This mystery that we live in our own inner, spiritual life is the same as that of the Church: "I saw the holy city and the new Jerusalem, coming down from God out of heaven, as beautiful as a bride all dressed for her husband" (Rv 21:2).

To "put on Christ" is to become a *new man*. When we contemplate Christ, we are transformed into him, the true new man, the new Adam whose features are alight with the personal presence of the son, God's image. "You have stripped off your old behavior with your old self, and you have put on a new self that will progress towards true knowledge the more it is renewed in the image of its creator" (Col 3:9-10). "You must put aside your old self...Your mind must be renewed by a spiritual revolution so that you can put on

239

the new self that has been created in God's way, in the goodness and holiness of the truth" (Eph 4:22-24; 2:15; 1 Cor 15:22; 15:44-49).

The spiritual man, recreated in us by Christ, lives in our hearts, and so we have the symbol of the *new heart*. "Shake off the sins you have committed against me, and make yourselves a new heart and a new spirit!" (Ez 18:31). "I shall give you a new heart, and put a new spirit in you; I shall remove the heart of stone from your bodies and give you a heart of flesh instead…you will be my people and I will be your God" (Ex 36:26-28).

The heart is very closely linked to the *spirit*. The Spirit lives in the hearts of men. He becomes the life and movement, the breath of life and the inspiration of our hearts. In Christ, the Spirit is essentially a Spirit of renewal, a personal presence dwelling in us and possessing us. We are no longer governed by exterior precepts but by an inner energy that has become our innermost self and our own creative freedom: "But now we are rid of the Law, freed by death from our imprisonment, free to serve in the new spiritual way and not the old way of a written law" (Rom 7:6).

And this is why Christ also brings an absolutely new *teaching*. It is not a new way of expressing the Old Law nor even a new content in the sense of its being a step forward in the discovery of realities hitherto unknown. In all reality Christ's teaching is a "spirit that gives life" (Jn 6:63). "Here is a teaching that is new, they said, and with authority behind it" (Mk 1:27). "Every scribe who becomes a disciple of the kingdom of heaven is like a householder who brings out from his storeroom things both old and new" (Mt 13:52). In this sense, every time we read the Bible something new occurs. On the level of the words that strike our senses, the "old man" in us has the impression of something well known and even hackneyed, but when we read it in the Spirit, we become, like the scribe of the kingdom, continually lost in admiration of what we discover.

Similarly, the *law* introduced by Jesus is totally new. Human behavior needs guidelines. Not only in the first stages of education, but from time to time throughout life we need to adjust our sights in Christ. But it is not a question simply of adjusting one's behavior to conform to an ideal. A Christian places his whole being under the guidance of the Spirit in truth and docility. We are no longer in search of an ideal but of a person whom we want to love. This is the wonderful newness of the Christian experience that reaches into the smallest details of our lives to change them. Charity is the only absolute. All else is relative, a means to something higher. These means can be lived according to the law by a sincere "natural" man; or they can be lived in the Spirit by the Christian. Just as there is a Christian way of sinning—quite literally—there is a Christian way of setting one's life in order. Both stand in relation to love. "Deep within them I will plant my Law, writing it on their hearts" (Jer 31:33).

Jesus expresses this in the new *commandment* he gives his disciples. It is not new because it is couched in new, more precise legal terms or because it is simpler or even because it is more demanding and more spiritual. Its newness lies in the fact that it is the gift of the Spirit who becomes the source of the new behavior required by the new commandment. "I give you a new commandment: love one another" (Jn 13:34). "This is *my* commandment: love one another, *as* I have loved you" (Jn 15:12). A new presence is necessary within man if he is to love *as* God loves. The law of the gospel and the new demands it makes in respect to forgiveness, conjugal fidelity and real poverty can only be understood in the context of love. They can only be lived in love. The Spirit has to be joined to our spirit to make us sharers in God's tender love.

When people are in love everything in creation is new. They learn the true language of the heart and can communicate with others and hear what they have to say on this level. This is what is symbolized by the *gift of tongues*, manifested in the first flush of the gift of the Spirit at Pentecost. Love, flooding into the world, enables all human beings to understand each other. "These are the signs that will be associated with believers . . . they will have the gift of tongues" (Mk 16:17). "They were all filled with the Holy Spirit, and began to speak foreign languages as the Spirit gave them the gift of speech" (Acts 2:4).

The Christian experience has also been expressed as a *way*, a new road. This was so often part of the early preaching of the apostles that the Christian community was dubbed "the Way" by their contemporaries (Acts 9:2; 18:25-26). It is new because it is "narrow" (Mt 7:13-14), whereas the "old man" instinctively prefers easy, spacious ways. But life is transmitted by a concentrated flow of life-forces, not by their scattering. To the Corinthians, longing for the thrill of spectacular charismata, Paul announces the way of charity, the "way that is better than any of them." (1 Cor 12:31). This is the way of love that our suffering and glorious Lord has opened for us. "Through the blood of Jesus we have the right to enter the sanctuary, by a new way which he has opened for us, a living opening through the curtain, that is to say, his body" (Heb 10:19-20). And here too the newness is in the fact that this way is someone, the Lord himself. "I am the Way...no one can come to the Father except through me" (Jn 14:6).

The way we take to the Father, in Jesus Christ, is the long journey to freedom that the Bible calls *Exodus*. Through the body of the risen Christ we can now live a new exodus. The one foretold by the second Isaiah during the Babylonian Captivity was never really accomplished until the coming of Christ. "See how former predictions have come true [the predictions that prepared the coming of Christ]. Fresh things I now foretell" (Is 42:9). In our spiritual experience no event is the exact replica of another, as is the case, for instance, in a psychological determinism. Every event is totally new because it involves us in a new exodus, a new departure from the land of our solitude toward an unprecedented self-giving in love. "No need to recall the past.... See, I am doing a new deed, even now it comes to light; can you not see it? Yes, I am making a road in the wilderness, paths in the wild" (Is 18-19). Christ is not just a way we follow, he is the very path we tread through the wilderness, the spiritual spring that quenches our thirst, and the bread that nourishes us in his body. He is the path that leads us out of our solitude into brotherly communion. If we live in him in a really personal way, we no longer wander in the desert of loneliness and death. Our daily life is a new exodus toward the land of the covenant.

This theme of the *new land* and the *new heavens* symbolizes the newness of others and, ultimately, of God. God and our neighbor are together and the new land in which we shall dwell. But we only reach this haven after much painful effort, and we can never settle down in it as long as we are still traveling the roads of the old earth. "For now I create new heavens and a new earth, and the past will not be remembered, and will come no more to men's minds" (Is 65:17). "For as the new heavens and the new earth I shall make endure before me, so will your race and name endure" (Is 66:22). "What we are waiting for is what he promised: the new heavens and new earth, the place where righteousness will be at home" (2 Pt 3:13). The newness of the risen Christ is the fact that the promised is no longer ahead of us but within us, already fulfilled. We have received the "pledge of our inheritance" (Eph 1:14), and when John sees "a new heaven and a new earth" (Rv 21:1) he is not seeing the universal restoration of the future but the beginning of the new creation in the risen body of the Lord. The Spirit of Christ introduces us into a life of resurrection which will be fully accomplished in the transformation of the universe.

The proof of this lies in the spiritual significance of the promised land. In the Old Testament it was already recognized that this was the land of the covenant. And now, living according to a new *covenant*, we have already entered the new land that is the heritage of the gentle and the peacemakers (Mt 5:4, 9). "This cup is the new covenant in my blood which shall be poured out for you" (Lk 22:20), "whenever you drink it, do this as a memorial of me.... Until the Lord comes, therefore, you are proclaiming his death" (1 Cor 11:25-27). Because we have our part and share in the blood of the Lord, we also share in his Spirit and in his life, and we have entered into a new homeland and a new dwelling place. "Until the Lord comes" the sacrament effects the passage from the old covenant, in which we were incapable of love, to the new, creative covenant by which we gain access into the mystery of another's being. Every time we refuse to be our own center of gravity and accept to enter into another's universe we actualize the coming of the Lord. The simplest act of love is pregnant with the blood of the Lord and with the light of his presence: every act of love is a parousia.

The same theme of mutual indwelling realized by the covenant helps us understand the theme of the *New Jerusalem*, capital of the kingdom established in love. The new Jerusalem is the very heart of the new human community we all yearn for, whether we be Christian or not. There can be no veritable brotherhood among men without a rebirth from the Father, and no authentic community without the indwelling presence of the One who is communion in men's hearts. At the end of his vision of universal restoration, Ezekiel glimpsed the new name of Jerusalem: "The name of the city in future is to be: Yahweh-is-there" (Ez 48:35). John, contemplating the risen Christ, goes even further: "I saw the holy city, and the new Jerusalem, coming from God out of heaven, as beautiful as a bride all dressed for her husband. Then I heard a loud voice call from the throne, "You see this city? Here lives God among men. He will make his home among them; they shall be his people, and he will be their God" (Rv 21:2-3).

The new Jerusalem is a mystery of presence and of communion, and this is why, in the heart of the new city, there must be a new Temple. "I saw that there was no temple in the city since the Lord God Almighty and the Lamb were themselves the temple" (Rv 21:22). All human dwellings fore-shadow and point to the new dwelling of personal interpenetration. If it is true that man is the Temple of God, it is also true that God is man's temple. "I am in my Father and you in me and I in you.... If anyone loves me...my Father will love him, and we shall come to him and make our home with him" (Jn 14:20, 23).

If the temple is radically new, the sacrifice also must be new. The new *sacrifice*, in a temple not built by the hands of man, is the Lamb, Christ, immolated and risen again, making perfect in one single offering all whom he sanctifies (Heb 10:12). To sacrifice, as we have seen, means to make holy, to sanctify or make sacred. All the sacrifices of the Old Testament and even those of the New Testament, in so far as they are external happenings, are "old." The newness introduced by the risen Christ is in the "spiritual revolution" (Eph 4:24) which turns the whole being into a self-offering. "Think of God's mercy, my brothers, and worship him, I beg you, in a way that is worthy of thinking beings, by offering your living bodies as a holy sacrifice, truly pleasing to God" (Rom 12:1).

This is why the wine and the blood of the old sacrifices can be expressed, in the blood of Christ, as the *new wine* of God's eternal vine. "From now on, I tell you, I shall not drink wine until the day I drink the new wine with you in the kingdom of my Father" (Mt 26:29). The new love feast supposed a complete renewal of our hearts: "Nor do people put new wine into old wineskins; if they do, the skins burst, the wine runs out, and the skins are lost. No; they put new wine into fresh skins and both are preserved" (Mt 9:17).

In the same way, the daily bread of charity requires that we become a new loaf of *bread*. "So get rid of all the old yeast, and make yourselves into a completely new batch of bread, unleavened as you are meant to be. Christ, our Passover, has been sacrificed" (1 Cor 5:7). The condition for participating in the Eucharistic meal is that we communicate with others "by getting rid of all the old yeast of evil and wickedness, having only the unleavened bread of sincerity and truth" (1 Cor 5:8).

In the Bible, as in life, a banquet is a symbol of rejoicing. Sharing in the new banquet inspires a new joy and a new *song* in our hearts. Authentic newness is a source of joy. This is expressed in the very word *gospel*, the "good news" or the "happy news." A person who lives according to the gospel sings a new song in his heart. It is not the juvenile enthusiasm of inexperience in which life is a beautiful day dream, it is the vigor of the adult who creates beauty in real life. Joy and the song that rises from the heart lie at the end of a pasch, an exodus, that is never fully accomplished on this earth. But since, in Christ, we can ceaselessly make the passage from egoism to love, from the absurd to life, we cannot help but sing, even while we suffer deeply. In the joy of the second exodus Isaiah exclaims: "Sing a new hymn to Yahweh! Let his praise resound from the ends of the earth" (Is 42:10; see also Ps 96:1; 149:1). And in the triumph of the final pasch, those who have risen with Christ sing the Song and can enter only through the risen Christ.

A renewal of joy is a sign of a renewal of life, and the integral experience of Christ in our lives is the experience of an ever new *life*. "When we were baptized we went into the tomb with him and joined him in death, so that as Christ was raised from the dead by the Father's glory, we too might live a new life" (Rom 6:4). "And we…all grow brighter and brighter as we are turned into the image that we reflect; this is the work of the Lord who is Spirit" (2 Cor 3:18).

Everything is transformed when it attains the maturity of its eternal being for which it has been groping ever since the first, faltering steps of creation. The biblical theme of newness emphasizes the interior renewal of man because God's newness enters the world by first entering into man in Christ. But just as the first appearance of man marks the summit of the evolution of matter, so man's fulfillment in the resurrection becomes the starting point of a new world. And the new world will, at last, be fully human because it will be overflowing with the fullness of God. When the whole of man and all men reach "their full stature in Christ" (Eph 4:13), then all things will reach the full maturity for which they were created. When the living, spiritual dwelling place of God in man and of man in God is perfected, then the whole *universe* will be renewed: "The world of the past has gone…. Now I am making the whole of creation new" (Rv 21:4-5).

PART FOUR

THE LITURGY OF LIFE

Life has reached out to all beings, and all
beings are filled with a great light....
Immortal and immense, the great Christ
shines over all beings more brilliantly than
the sun. And so, for us who believe in him, a
day has dawned, all of light, long and eternal,
a day that will never end, our mystic Pasch.

—St. Hippolytus

CHAPTER ELEVEN

The Liturgy, Unity in Love

Religious rationalism, which all too often takes the place of a Christian experience in people's lives, does nothing to prepare the believer in the modern world for the newness of the resurrection. Instinctively, unable to deal with it, many people prefer to ignore it, like the Athenians of the Areopagus (Acts 17). In fact one of our greatest temptations is to try to attenuate the disconcerting aspects of this novelty in our thoughts and actions and to bring it within the accepted categories of human knowledge. It is already a big step forward from a knowledge of the God of philosophy when we discover the living God. But it is a far greater step—and one that has to be taken repeatedly—to experience the living God as resurrection. The newness that Christ introduced is contained in the resurrection. Our salvation, or in other words the full flowering of our human vocation, lies not simply in the living God but in the risen Christ in whom we live in a very real way.

The rationalist "believer" feels a similar estrangement in regard to the liturgy and the sacraments, wholly unknown to, and considered utopian by, the scientific and technical minds. C. G. Jung and his followers have hardly begun to reconcile modern man with the unexplored, despised terrain of the unconscious. Not that the Christian experience of liturgy is simply an expression of the collective unconscious, although there is no doubt that its roots in human psychology lie in this direction. Even if a man finally arrives at a point where he is able to reintegrate the world of symbols, socially and psychologically, into his conscious life, he will still not have crossed the threshold of the Christian liturgical mystery. God is resurrection and cannot be equated with the living God of Jewish monotheism. In the same way Christian liturgy is resurrection, and it cannot be equated with the fulfillment of the need for ritual of the human psyche. It contains a dimension that is totally new and into which we can enter only through the risen Christ.

The full meaning of the existence of every Christian lies in being a witness to the God-event present in the risen Christ, and every Christian should be able to say, with Paul, "I have without faltering put before you the whole of God's purpose" (Acts 20:27). Paul's experimental knowledge of God's purpose embraces the story of his own life and apostleship, starting with the revelation of the whole Christ on the road to Damascus and including the realization that his return is imminent, the work of organizing the churches, and the new appreciation he gained of Christian faith and freedom culminating in his experience of the fullness of Christ during his captivity. At the end of his life, Paul prefers to use the word "mystery," including in this one word the whole of God's plan of salvation. This is the mystery expressed so beautifully in the prologue of his letter to the Ephesians. But it is precisely when God's plan is revealed in its entirety that it becomes liturgy. And when we seek to live it in its entirety, our life becomes a celebration of his mystery; in other words our life becomes liturgy.

This is the keynote in John's revelation. Everything is contained in the Alpha and Omega, the beginning and the end. If the Christian experience is the apocalyptic experience of the Book of Revelation, then it is one great liturgy. For is not John's vision the revelation of Christ, Christ who *is* the liturgy of the universe and of time, who *is* the restoration of all things in love, who *is the* flood tide of interpersonal communion sweeping away all the obstacles of our native pettiness? In Christ, introducing a new creation in his new body, God reveals himself to be resurrection. In Christ, capturing all time in one eternal liturgy, God reveals himself to be the true adoration of all history. This is not a figure of speech by which we are attributing to a personification of history the adoration of which the hearts of men are capable, but the inner reality of history in which we live and which we have to bring to fruition. In the risen Christ history reaches its climax in the transparency of a personal wonderment. Christ embraces everything common to mankind, including the dimension of time. The adoration of history is time "restored to life" in Christ and turning back to its own source, the Father, in a liturgy of praise.

GOD'S PLAN IS A LITURGY

The most obscure pages of the Bible are, no doubt, those that speak an apocalyptic language. There are many in the prophets: Ezekiel (38, 39) and the post-exilic prophets such as Isaiah (24–27; 63–66), Zechariah (9–14) and Daniel (7–12). The New Testament has such passages in Matthew (24, 25), Mark (13), Luke (21), Thessalonians (2:3-8) and, of course, the Book of Revelation. It seems that the apocalyptic style is an integral part of the development of the prophetic ministry. The prophet's task is to "reveal" the meaning of events through the proclamation of God's world or to reveal his "presence" (parousia) in events. Prophecy is not simply a moral teaching geared to history. As the revelation of the living God develops, it becomes more and more self-evident that the whole of history, and not only contemporary events, are illuminated by his presence. And as the Prophets of the Old Testament came closer to God's coming in the flesh, the realization that the whole of history is part of God's plan became clearer. With the coming of Jesus, all the apocalyptic prophecies are fulfilled once and for all, but embryonically. The unfolding in time of what is already contained in him leaves ample scope for the further clarifications contained in the Christian teaching of the gospels and in the Book of Revelation.

But it should be remarked that John's Revelation, interwoven as it is with the events of the first struggle between the Church and the Prince of this world and studded with references reminiscent of the prophets, unfolds in the form of a liturgy. Let us look at the origin and meaning of this word, *liturgy*. In the Greek translation of the Old Testament, the word is habitually used to render various Hebrew terms having to do with the cult. It means the "ministry" or service of the priests and Levites (Ez 38:21). In the New Testament this meaning is extended—even to the point of including the service of a public office (Rom 13:6)—to mean the function of "sacralizing" all human activity. The liturgy is a "holy service" (2 Cor 9:13). Finally, it is the "ministry" of the High Priest, Christ (Heb 8:6), the supreme "priestly duty" of the new covenant (Heb 10:11; 8:2), which the apostles accomplish when they proclaim the gospel (Rom 15:16).

"God has given me this special position. He has appointed me as a priest of Jesus Christ, and I am to carry out my priestly duty by bringing the Good News from God to the pagans, and so make them acceptable as an offering, made holy by the Holy Spirit" (Rom 15:16). This text carries us to the very heart of God's plan. The *promise* that prefigures this plan is summed up in the covenant and the kingdom reached through a pasch. And, as we have seen, the whole meaning of the *Pasch* and of the *Exodus* from Egypt is in the goal: to offer a cult to God on this mountain (Ex 3:12). Paul also speaks of the freedom into which the paschal journey leads as a service in love (Gal 5:13). On the other hand, we have seen that the mystery of the covenant and the kingdom is something more than the sociological phenomenon. It is God's gift of love to humanity, a sacerdotal communion. We are a "royal priesthood" (Ex 19:16; 1 Pt 2:4-10). If the kingdom is the irruption of the new creation into the world of the first creation, one can see that the mystery of the whole of creation is a liturgy, starting with the first image of God in man and reaching fulfillment through the unity of all humanity in the risen Christ (Col 1:15 f; 1 Cor 15:28).

If the redemption did not culminate in a liturgy, it would be a gift of God that leaves man forever within his own orbit. The communion between God and man and between men, in Christ, is open only in the attitude of offering that is the liturgical attitude. If our pasch were not set on this course we would necessarily fall back within our own narrow horizons. But our Christian experience is a continual upward and outward movement, beyond the pull of gravity that is death, in the immense pasch that reaches from the beginning to the end of the world and of time. In this paschal thrust the cosmic dimensions of reality reach fulfillment in man, biological reality reaches fulfillment in the human person, sociological reality is perfected in the communion of persons, and the psychological reality flowers in the gratuitousness of love. All of man and all men reach fulfillment in Christ, and Christ in God. "So there is nothing to boast about in anything human . . . the world, life and death, the present and the future, are all your servants; but you belong to Christ and Christ belongs to God" (1 Cor 3:21-23). The liturgy is the disintegration of all negations in the ever-new openness of communion in the Trinity.

But one thing is important: liturgy is a "sacred service." Christ's pasch, which encompasses all things from the first atom to the fullness of the kingdom, is not a continuous, unfaltering movement of universal evolution, blindly and inevitably reaching fulfillment in God. History is the battlefield on which the liberty of God, of man and of Satan come to grips. The thrust of creation is trammeled by man's sin.

And liturgy is "sacrifice," and mankind is a "priesthood" because that which is no longer holy must be restored to holiness, and life must be restored through and beyond death. Christ's resurrection is the sacrifice which encompasses all the abortive efforts of life groping for expression. The Cross was the "service" by which man gives himself up totally to God and which thereby becomes his liberation. It is still this for us. If Easter is the "panegyric of the whole of creation," as Hippolytus says, it is not in the sense of a natural apotheosis, but in the sense that, purified by death of all that is not love, personal beings have reached a lifestyle of total oblation, have become "a living sacrifice" (Rom 12:1), a "royal priesthood" (1 Pt 2:9). The final goal and meaning of all things is to love, but love only exists in a climate of self-giving and in the praise of God's glory (Eph 1:6, 12, 14).

THE MYSTERY IN THE LAST DAYS

All that is revealed by the Bible of the resurrection and of liturgy is eloquent proof that our Christian experience is the experience of beings who are *already* risen from death. We can never be too strongly convinced of this radical newness. "You have been brought back to true life with Christ . . . and now the life you have is hidden with Christ in God" (Col 3:1-3). "We are already the children of God" (1 Jn 3:2). In Christ, the God-event fills all history. That which happened once for all (Heb 9:26) is contemporary to all of time and space. "By virtue of that one single offering, he has achieved the eternal perfection of all whom he is sanctifying" (Heb 10:14). Our Christian experience is one of plentitude. Even time is raised from the dead. It is no longer simply a quantitative measurement of change, it is the qualitative newness of "now" overflowing with a presence. Time has become the stuff of grace, the place where the gift of his presence meets our response.

This fullness of presence does not abolish the movement of time. On the contrary, it increases its momentum. It does not freeze history at any given point, but opens it all to maturity. The pivotal Christ-event does not void all that has gone before, whether in the unfolding of the centuries or in human mentalities. On the contrary, everything that is "before his time," whether in history or in our hearts, takes on depth and consistency as a preparation for his coming, the beginning of the way that opens out in him, "God-With-Us" (Rv 21:3). Nor does the Christ-event void what comes after him. Time goes on, but with a new energy content of resurrection that sets it in a new orbit. Since Christ's resurrection, history moves forward from the "appointed time" to the time of "accomplishment," accomplishment of God's mystery (Rv 10:7), of the faith that gave us birth (Heb 12:2) and above all, of love, the seed of God growing in us (Jn 17:23). Since Christ rose and recapitulated all things in himself, the quality of time has changed radically for every man and for every human community. One can still speak of "an Old Testament mentality" even in certain Christians, in Muslims or people of other religions or of no religion, but this is only valid by comparison. In fact, whatever attitude a man may have, we are all henceforth living in a total context in which the risen Christ is the axial, determining factor, even if this is not visibly so. The passage from the fullness of time to its accomplishment involves and includes all who are actually living.

We are living, now, in the period that the gospel calls the "last days" (1 Cor 10:11). The word "last" must be taken in a qualitative, not a quantitative sense, meaning that nothing substantially new lies in the future since "all newness" is *already* with us in Christ. Once the living seed is present, the fruit is already present even if it is *not yet* apparent. The paradox of the last days lies in the coexistence of the "already" and of the "not yet" of God's presence (Col 1:22) and of this present world (Ti 2:12). We are living both "in the flesh," that is, in the weakness of man-in-himself and "in the Spirit," that is, in the strength of the new man. *Pentecost inaugurated a new type of man, a new humanism* in which the last remnants of ambiguity are swept away. Mortal man will live forever, even in the body; egoistical man will love forever; man torn by inner conflict will find an indestructible unity; man, the sinner, will be transformed in God's holiness. The paradoxical situation is expressed in the beatitudes (Mt 5:3f): the poor become rich, the gentle inherit the earth, the afflicted rejoice because wealth, power and joy have become realities of a new order, the order of the Spirit fulfilling and correcting the original human condition.

The times we live since the springtime of the resurrection are times of a slow and patient growth (Lk 8:15; 2 Pt 3:8). It is the period that lies between the decisive moment in which, in Christ, all humanity entered into God's fullness (Eph 2:6) and the moment in which each one of us enters into this fullness by the free welcome he gives to Christ, Savior. It is a period in which the Evil One, although he is already conquered, is not reduced to impotence. It is a time of witness in which we, who must bear witness to the resurrection, have to account to all men for the hope that lies in us: "This Good News will be proclaimed to the whole world as a witness to all the nations. And then the end will come" (Mt 24:14). "Always have your answer ready for people who ask you the reason for the hope you all have" (1 Pt 3:15). "The Lord is not being slow to carry out his promises, as anybody else might be called slow; but he is being patient with you all, wanting nobody to be lost and everybody to be brought to change his ways" (2 Pt 3:9). We are living in the unfolding of an epiphany, an apocalypse in which everything is already present, growing toward the final perfect manifestation. "You have died, and now the life you have is hidden with Christ in God. But when Christ is revealed—and he is your life—you too will be revealed in all your glory with him" (Col 3:3-4). "My dear people, we are already the children of God but what we are to be in the future has not yet been revealed" (1 Jn 3:2).

THE LITURGY OF THE LAST DAYS

How can we make the resurrection our own on a truly personal level? In the last chapter we saw how God's plan concerning the mediation of love is revealed in the theme of Israel's homecoming. This is the mystery of the Church as instrument of salvation, as a people chosen as God's envoys: "All the tribes of the earth shall bless themselves by you" (Gn 12:3). Every part of the reality of the present-day Church exists within the mystery of priesthood: "You are a royal priesthood" (1 Pt 2:9). The functions of the teaching Magisterium, as well as the pastoral jurisdiction, are essentially priestly. The Church, since it is the Body of Christ the High Priest and the Temple of the sanctifying Spirit, is a

sacramental mediation between God and man. This mediation consists in bringing the power of the resurrection to bear
on all things, in all spheres.

During the forty days that lay between Christ's entry
into the glory of the Father and his resurrection and his exal-
tation over the world by his ascension, he introduced his
apostles to the new manner in which he was present amongst
them. The forty days are the fulfillment of Exodus, symbolizing the wilderness through which the new People of God
march toward the heavenly Jerusalem. "For forty days he
had continued to appear to them and tell them about the kingdom of God" (Acts 1:3-4). The teaching of Jesus, at this junc-
ture, turned on two main points: a biblical catechesis and a
liturgical event. Jesus initiates his disciples into a "Christian"
understanding of the Old Testament by pointing out "what
concerned him" (Lk 24:27) in Moses, the Prophets and the
Psalms. "He then opened their minds to understand the scriptures" (Lk 24:45). But we know from the earliest preaching of
the Church (Acts 1:40) that his apparitions and his teaching
usually occurred in connection with a meal (Lk 24:30-32;
24:40-42; Mk 15:14; Jn 21:12-14; Acts 1:3-4). These events are
of first importance—after the actual establishment of the
Eucharist at the Last Supper—for the experience of the presence of the risen Christ in the first Christian communities (1
Cor 11; see also Rv 3:20). During these forty days, symbol of
the present time of the Church, Jesus taught his disciples
that he was present with them in a new way in "the Lord's
Supper" (1 Cor 11:20).

The whole life of the Church, therefore, is present in
the eucharistic liturgy, since the Church is communion in the

Body of Christ, and the Eucharist is the locus of Christ's glorious presence in the world. All of history is here present. It is truly the *memorial* of the pasch by which all humanity is on the way to the Father; it is the *Presence* of the Lord in the life of the Church; finally, it is *anticipation* of his return, "until the Lord comes" (1 Cor 11:26). The most ancient Christian prayer, "Lord, come!" ("Maranatha," 1 Cor 16:22; Rv 22:20) is answered in the eucharistic meal, "For where two or three meet in my name, I shall be there with them" (Mt 18:20; see also the *Didache* 10:6). Christ's presence is not simply a "moral" presence, or one that is only the memory of his friends. It is the absolutely real, "paschal" presence of the only son of God, who "having loved those of his who were in the world" now shows "how perfect his love was" (Jn 13:1).

The risen Christ can be sacramentally present in the world since he is no longer the Christ we know "according to the flesh." His humanity is with the Father, and he cannot be present in the same manner now as during his life on earth. But his sacramental presence is not a sort of absence. Jesus became incarnate forever, not just for thirty years. He will always be "in" the world without being "of" the world. The sacraments—and the eucharistic liturgy is the supreme sacrament—are precisely the manner in which the risen Christ has elected to be present in the world, although he is no longer of the world.

We must interpret the "signs" related in John's Gospel in the light of his existence after rising from the dead. The sacraments are God's signs today, and the miracle of the wine at Cana and the multiplication of the loaves point unequivocally to the eucharistic sign. In them the risen

Christ manifests his "glory" (Jn 2:11, 22; 11:4, 40). And his glory is the same glory that radiates from the cross and the resurrection (Jn 1:14; 12:16). Jesus' "hour" of glory (Jn 12:23; 13:31) is made present sacramentally, therefore, whenever Christians come together to celebrate the new "day of the Lord." In the breaking of bread he who is risen from the dead is present amongst us. Those who heard Jesus' words about the Bread of Life at Capharnaum were scandalized because they could only imagine that he was advocating some kind of cannibalistic rite. But Jesus warns them that his words can only be understood in the light of his resurrection. "Does this upset you? What if you should see the Son of Man ascend to where he was before? It is the spirit that gives life, the flesh has nothing to offer" (Jn 6:62-63). When we come together for the Lord's Supper (1 Cor 11:20) we "eat his flesh and drink his blood" (Jn 6:53) because he is risen. We eat the spiritual body of the second Adam who comes from heaven (1 Cor 15:44-47), as Jesus said of the Bread of Life (Jn 6:33). But we do so in the sign of the bread and the wine of the Last Supper when Christ delivered himself up for the life of the world. And so this meal is at the same time the *memorial* of his passion, the actualization of his *presence* of resurrection and the *anticipation* of his return in glory, since his first coming is the beginning of his final coming.

And so we can say that as the whole Christian experience is the experience of the whole Christ, the point at which this experience reaches a mysterious fullness and perfection is in the liturgy. The different steps in God's design, into which are intertwined the mystery of Christ, become personal in application to each one of us and present in the liturgy. To communicate in the eucharistic liturgy is to receive into oneself the dynamic of the pasch, foreshadowed in the Old Testament and accomplished once for all in the cross and the resurrection.

It follows that Christian spirituality is essentially liturgical. It is the dynamic of the Spirit present in the "last days" in which we are living. In the liturgy we live the "already" of the coming of the kingdom; we have access to the resurrection: "Anyone who does eat my flesh and drink my blood has eternal life" (Jn 6:54). Man becomes once again the priest of all creation, bringing all things to perfection in the freedom of God's children. God's love springs up in an inexhaustible newness. And the loving adoration of all history is expressed in the personal offering man makes of himself in Christ. And at the same time the liturgy is the experience of the "not yet" of the kingdom. Christ is the path that God's patience lays before man and by which he can always come home to the Father. The liturgy is not only the adoration offered to God by men who have been saved. It is also the gift of mercy held out to those who are not yet saved. It is not only the goal of the pasch, it is also the momentum that carries it forward.

In the liturgy, a Christian can test the authenticity of his commitment (1 Cor 11:28). The liturgical experience demands an effective charity at work *in* the world to be saved, just as it demands a holiness that is "scandal" because it is not *of* this world.

But if Christian spirituality is liturgical, this also means that it is both theocentric and missionary. The mystical and the moral cannot be dissociated since the Christian being is sacramental in nature.

Finally, all the paradoxes of our dual condition are resolved in harmony around the pole of the liturgical drama. We are risen from death with Christ, but we are still the sacraments of his coming, and from this flows the practice of faith, hope, obedience, poverty, chastity and all the social aspects of the Church. These are the values that announce the coming of the eternal kingdom, and yet they are all destined to disappear: only love will remain (1 Cor 13).

CONCLUSION

THE SYMPHONY OF THE WORD

In the mystery of the incarnate Word lies the
power of the symbols and figures of Scripture
as well as the knowledge of all creatures

—Maximus the Confessor

In the Christian experience all is Christ, the word of God, and it is he who, at the very first notes of creation, accords his instrument to ours in order to lead all things to the final, triumphant symphony of eternity, of which the Bible is the score. Our integral experience unfolds in successive themes and variations, constantly resolving into new melodic movements. *Creation* is the prelude of this vast, orchestral work, and the theme of it is the first gratuitousness in which the word makes himself available to our inner being. Through the *promise* he comes into our lives and awakens us to liberty in faith. From this flows the movement toward liberty of the whole of creation in the *Pasch* of the incarnate Word, rising in a crescendo of love and climaxing in the full conquest of freedom in our own *exodus*. At the end of this movement we reach the peace of God's interiority, the *covenant*, and the interiority of man, the *kingdom*. *Already* the symphony of the word ushers us into God's eternal day, for all is accomplished when one lives in truth. And yet sin and death are still at work in man and in the world. We have *not yet* reached the full harmony of love. And so the themes of the first movement are taken up in a minor key: the *Exile* reiterates the theme of the promise, strengthening us in our freedom to give; the *Return* echoes the theme of the power of life inherent in Christ's first pasch and our first exodus. Our original experience of the covenant and of the kingdom becomes a hymn of *Resurrection*. And finally, in the last movement, when the word of God takes to himself the final dimension of our mortal condition, the symphony of the human and the divine becomes the eternal *Liturgy*.

The liturgy sings the birth of new life springing from Christ on the cross. Our experience, in him, becomes an experience of *unity*. Unity of matter and spirit, of the "psychic" and the spiritual, of the mystery of persons and the mystery of history, unity of our liberated selves with our fellows in the communion of God with man. Because Christ brings all things together in personal communion, no aspect of our existence is left out. Everything has a meaning and comes to fruition in the victory of love. Life and death, pain and joy, fugitive time and the eternity that already dwells in us, failure and success, our sin and our repentance, all have their note to sing in the supreme liturgy of the eternal pasch. Through the Bible, we can follow the orchestral crescendo as it unfolds on the different levels of our experience: the development of our own personality, the apprenticeship of relations with others, the growth of human community, the realization of the meaning of history. The ten major themes of the biblical score encompass the main theme, the variations and the whole orchestration of all human life.

This is why we can in all honesty say that the Christian experience, even now, is an experience of full *perfection* (Gal 4:4; Eph 1:23; Col 1:19). The Christian, *if he really lives as a Christian*, is in constant communion with all men and with all that is human, developing within himself and spreading abroad by his very lifestyle the hope that encourages his fellows. He is far more truly in the service of man and an architect of history than any Marxist. He is more deeply immersed in existence than the existentialists; more exacting and more faithful than the integral conservatives; richer in new ideas than the progressives. He is more realistic than the rationalists and more clear-sighted than any pessimist. He feels in his bones that all the paths that men have taken to reach God, from the sophisticated codes of the great religions to the inarticulate belief of animists, pass through his body and soul. He knows that his solidarity with them has reached unimaginable depths in Christ, and that this means that he must go all the way with them on their road to fulfillment. This fullness of "recapitulation" (Eph 1:10) that Christ has lived, once for all time in his person, becomes our life too when the Bible enters our lives in the sacramental liturgy. Then our whole being and existence becomes a liturgy of salvation for mankind and of adoration of God.

At the beginning of his commentary on the Song of Songs, Origen reminds us that before we sing this song, we must first of all learn to sing all the others, from the Song of Moses to that of Isaiah. He then speaks of six preliminary, spiritual stages, each of which is characterized by a song.

These correspond to the principal stages in the Christian experience that we have explored in this book. The Song of Liberation (Ex 15) corresponds to the experience of the *pasch*; that of the well (Nm 21:17) is the song of the *Exodus* through the desert. The great Song of Moses, within sight of the promised land, is the song of the *covenant* (Dt 32). The first song of the land (Jgs 5) sings of the conquest, the "not yet" of the *kingdom*, whereas the second (2 Sm 22) sings of peace, the "already" of the kingdom. In the Song of the Vineyard (Is 5) is contained the spiritual drama of the *exile*. Only then can we reach the Song of Songs which sings of the mystery of the *return*, the fulfillment of the eternal covenant.

Creation and *promise* are marked by no special songs in the Bible. At this stage everything is still a seed hidden in the ground. It is only when the harvest is gathered that the people sing. Psalm 126 is the song of the harvest because it is the song of the return: "They went away, went away weeping, carrying the seed; they come back, come back singing, carrying their sheaves." The first song rises from the fullness of man's heart when he is set free (Ex 15); it is the pasch. The last song, the song that will last forever and be eternally a "new song," will rise from the hearts of all men and all creation in the radiant newness of God, when he has become "all things to all men." The Song of Moses will become the song of the Lamb (Rv 15:1-4), and this is the eternal covenant: "They shall be his people, and he will be their God; his name is God-with-them. He will wipe away all tears from their eyes; there will be no more death, and no more mourning or sadness. The world of the past has gone.... Now I am making the whole of creation new" (Rv 21:3-5).

INDEX